New Approaches to Family Pastoral Care

Douglas A. Anderson

Fortress Press   Philadelphia

Creative Pastoral Care and Counseling Series
Editor: Howard J. Clinebell, Jr.
Associate Editor: Howard W. Stone

The Care and Counseling of Youth in the Church by Paul B. Irwin
Growth Counseling for Marriage Enrichment: Pre-Marriage and the Early Years by Howard J. Clinebell, Jr.
Crisis Counseling by Howard W. Stone
Pastoral Care and Counseling in Grief and Separation by Wayne E. Oates
Counseling for Liberation by Charlotte Holt Clinebell
Growth Counseling for Mid-Years Couples by Howard J. Clinebell, Jr.
Theology and Pastoral Care by John B. Cobb, Jr.
Pastor and Parish—A Systems Approach by E. Mansell Pattison
Pastoral Care with Handicapped Persons by Lowell G. Colston
Care and Counseling of the Aging by William M. Clements
Anger and Assertiveness in Pastoral Care by David W. Augsburger
Using Behavioral Methods in Pastoral Counseling by Howard W. Stone
New Approaches to Family Pastoral Care by Douglas A. Anderson

Biblical quotations from the Revised Standard Version of the Bible, copyright 1946, 1952, © 1971, 1973 by the Division of Christian Education of the National Council of the Churches of Christ in the U.S.A., are used by permission.

"The Tale of the Sands" in chapter 1 is from *Tales of the Dervishes* by Idries Shah. Copyright © 1967 by Idries Shah. Reprinted by permission of the publisher, E. P. Dutton.

Library of Congress Cataloging in Publication Data

Anderson, Douglas A   1939–
New approaches to family pastoral care.

(Creative pastoral care and counseling series)
Bibliography: p.
1. Family—Religious life.   2.   Pastoral theology.   I.   Title.
BV4526.2.A52   253'.5   79–8898
ISBN 0–8006–0564–0

8020J80   Printed in the United States of America   1–564

Contents

65330

Series Foreword

Let me share with you some of the hopes that are in the minds of those of us who helped to develop this series—hopes that relate directly to you as the reader. It is our desire and expectation that these books will be of help to you in developing better working tools as a minister-counselor. We hope that they will do this by encouraging your own creativity in developing more effective methods and programs for helping people live life more fully. It is our intention in this series to affirm the many things you have going for you as a minister in helping troubled persons—the many assets and resources from your religious heritage, your role as the leader of a congregation, and your unique relationship to individuals and families throughout the life cycle. We hope to help you reaffirm the *power of the pastoral* by the use of fresh models and methods in your ministry.

The aim of the series is not to be comprehensive with respect to topics but rather to bring innovative approaches to some major types of counseling. Although the books are practice-oriented, they also provide a solid foundation of theological and psychological insights. They are written primarily for ministers (and those preparing for the ministry) but we hope that they will also prove useful to other counselors who are interested in the crucial role of spiritual and value issues in all helping relationships. In addition we hope that the series will be useful in seminary courses, clergy support groups, continuing education workshops, and lay befriender training.

This is a period of rich new developments in counseling and

psychotherapy. The time is ripe for a flowering of creative methods and insights in pastoral care and counseling. Our expectation is that this series will stimulate grass-roots creativity as innovative methods and programs come alive for you. Some of the major thrusts that will be discussed in this series include a new awareness of the unique contributions of the theologically trained counselor, the liberating power of the human potentials orientation, an appreciation of the pastoral care function of the ministering congregation, the importance of humanizing systems and institutions as well as close relationships, the importance of pastoral *care* (and not just counseling), the many opportunities for caring ministries throughout the life cycle, the deep changes in male-female relationships, and the new psychotherapies such as Gestalt therapy, Transactional Analysis, educative counseling, and crisis methods. Our hope is that this series will enhance your resources for your ministry to persons by opening doorways to understanding of these creative thrusts in pastoral care and counseling.

In this book on family change Douglas Anderson shares his broad knowledge and extensive experience as a family therapist and as a facilitator of marriage and family enrichment. He describes a fresh, exciting approach to helping families through pastoral care and counseling. His central theme is that each family has a guiding image or metaphor by which they understand and respond to the world. Their metaphor can either block or enable needed change within the family as they relate to each other and to the world. At each stage of a family life cycle their guiding metaphor needs updating to enable them to cope with the new problems and use the new possibilities of that era. In Anderson's view, the continuing transformation of a family's metaphor is the key to helping them change so that they can handle the changes in society as well as in the new situation they face with the passing years.

The transformation of family metaphors often occurs as a family, after strenuous human efforts, lets go and allows the transcendent Spirit to carry them to a new place. The Spirit can speak to family members who are seeking new images through another family, a pastor, or a counselor. The process through which this happens can best be enabled by using metaphoric communication.

After presenting five basic principles of family transformation and tracing the changing metaphors of the stages of a particular family's life cycle, the author describes eight techniques of metaphoric communication: active imagination; stories, parables, dreams; reframing a problem; aphorisms, jokes, and ambiguities; creative memories; action imperatives; affirmations; and play (including finger painting, drawing, dancing, and dramatizing!). He then shows in very practical ways how to use these eight techniques in marriage and family enrichment and in pastoral family therapy. The book uses abundant case illustrations, including some from the author's own family experience. Anderson practices what he teaches us by including vivid metaphoric tales at the beginning and end of the book. He shows how an understanding of metaphoric communication can open up important insights concerning the meaning and uses of the biblical "word."

Earlier in his career Douglas Anderson was for a while a parish pastor. He then served on the staff of three pastoral counseling centers. At present he is a pastoral counselor on the staff of Lutheran Social Services of the state of Washington. His professional time is divided among three areas: counseling and therapy, mainly marriage and family therapy; training family therapists and educators; and doing preventive family education, mainly marriage and family enrichment. His chief career interest in all these activities is enhancing the quality of living in our human relationships, particularly the family. Doug and his wife Joan (also a trained marriage and family therapist) colead marriage and family enrichment events and are busy "growing our own marriage and family relationships," which are very important to them.

As I first read the typescript of this book, I had a series of "aha!" experiences. My energy level rose as I sensed an innovative and practical application of right-brain research to an area of pastoral care in which it will come like gentle rain on parched earth. For those of us who were trained mainly in left-brain oriented counseling and therapy (which is analytical, interpretive, and rational) the central thrust of this book will provide access to the complementary and much-needed "other side" of the healing-growthing art. I predict that this book will be used by a wide variety of people—parish pastors, lay parish carers, pastoral counseling specialists, marriage and family therapists, and, perhaps most important of all, parents and other family members who are engaged in creating new family metaphors. As you read the book, I hope that you will find yourself examining your own guiding images and perhaps experiencing (as this reader did) the awareness of their gradual transformation. The author says that he is excited about the approaches described in these pages. So am I! My hope and expectation is that you too will become excited as you discover new resources for crossing the deserts on your own journey and the journeys of families with whom you minister.

HOWARD J. CLINEBELL, JR.

What Is in This Book

The children in our family, Duane and Mark, can hardly wait at Christmas for my wife, Joan, and me to open the presents they have bought us and wrapped themselves. They wait eagerly for us to take off the wrapping and see what is inside each box. I feel that same kind of eagerness as you open the cover of this book and discover what is inside.

What is in this book is something old and something new. The something old is a reminder of the ancient traditions and resources of the church for assisting families through the passages of their journey through the human life cycle. The something new is a connecting of these resources with contemporary psychology's rediscovery of the therapeutic power of communicating with the right hemisphere of the human brain, the metaphoric mind.

Down the centuries the church has strengthened families through sharing bread for their life journey. The bread it has offered includes the Bible with its family stories, figurative language, and vivid images of myths and parables; the rabbi/priest or pastor who shares healing wisdom through storytelling and counsel; the rituals, symbols, and sacraments which mark and enlighten life's passages from birth to death; the community of families who undergird each other with sustaining power; and the Holy Spirit who breathes life-giving energy into these words, rabbis, rituals, and communities.

Contemporary psychology has awakened fresh interest in the imaginative, intuitive, creative capacities of the metaphoric mind. New tools are being developed to communicate directly with this facet of the mind in order to facilitate change in persons and families. These tools abound with potential for application to the church's ministry to families.

This book is addressed to ministers and lay leaders who seek to strengthen families within the context of the church. The aim of the book is to enable you to utilize creatively the church's resources and the tools of metaphoric-mind communication in facilitating family growth through the life cycle. I intend to present a model for family change, specify a number of tools for metaphorical communication, and apply the model and the tools to the practice of three forms of ministry to families: marriage and family enrichment, family life cycle education, and pastoral family therapy.

I am excited about these approaches. They have enriched my life as a family member and as a minister to families through education and counseling. I hope that what I have written will open some new possibilities for you where you live and minister.

I want to express my appreciation to Joan Anderson, Terry Gibson, and Don Smith for reading the manuscript and giving helpful suggestions, and to Joan and Bernadine Anderson who typed the manuscript. Finally, I am grateful to all the families who have been my teachers.

1. Family Transformation

A stream, from its source in far-off mountains, passing through every kind and description of countryside, at last reached the sands of the desert. Just as it had crossed every other barrier, the stream tried to cross this one, but it found that as fast as it ran into the sand, its waters disappeared.

It was convinced, however, that its destiny was to cross this desert, and yet there was no way. Now a hidden voice, coming from the desert itself, whispered, "The Wind crosses the desert, and so can the stream."

The stream objected that it was dashing itself against the sand and only getting absorbed, that the Wind could fly, and this was why it could cross a desert.

"By hurtling in your own accustomed way you cannot get across. You will either disappear or become a marsh. You must allow the Wind to carry you over, to your destination."

But how could this happen? "By allowing yourself to be absorbed in the Wind."

This idea was not acceptable to the stream. After all, it had never been absorbed before. It did not want to lose its individuality. And, once having lost it, how was one to know that it could ever be regained?

"The Wind," said the sand, "performs this function. It takes up water, carries it over the desert, and then lets it fall again. Falling as rain, the water again becomes a river."

"How can I know that this is true?"

"It is so, and if you do not believe it, you cannot become more than a quagmire, and even that could take many, many years; and it certainly is not the same as a stream."

"But can I not remain the same stream that I am today?"

"You cannot in either case remain so," the whisper said. "Your essential part is carried away and forms a stream again. You are called what you are even today because you do not know which part of you is the essential one."

1

When he heard this, certain echoes began to arise in the thoughts of the stream. Dimly he remembered a state in which he—or some part of him, was it?—had been held in the arms of a Wind. He also remembered—or did he?—that this was the real thing, not necessarily the obvious thing, to do.

And the stream raised his vapor into the welcoming arms of the Wind, which gently and easily bore it upwards and along, letting it fall softly as soon as they reached the roof of a mountain many, many miles away. And because he had had his doubts, the stream was able to remember and record more strongly in his mind the details of the experience. He reflected, "Yes, now I have learned my true identity."

The stream was learning. But the sands whispered, "We know because we see it happen day after day and because we, the sands, extend from the riverside all the way to the mountain."

And that is why it is said that the way in which the Stream of Life is to continue on its journey is written in the Sands.*

Idries Shah's "Tale of the Sands" is a beautiful story in its simplicity and power. I believe that through its metaphoric language it also communicates several important truths about families. Five of these truths or principles have important implications for those of us who seek to minister creatively to families in the context of the church:

1. Families are moving, changing, developing entities. Families do not stand still. Like bubbling streams they are forever changing their shape and tempo as they journey through the hills, valleys, and plateaus that compose the stages of the family life cycle.

2. Families frequently get blocked when they come to a new passageway in the life cycle journey. Entering a "desert" brings new tasks and opportunities that require new approaches. Families often get bogged down by repetitively trying to apply approaches that worked in former stages but that do not fit the new situation. They futilely dash themselves against the desert sand.

3. Families change by finding a new way through the formerly blocked passageway. The desert can be crossed if the stream is transformed into clouds and rain. Creative resources inside and outside families are utilized in a process which transforms families while at the same time preserving their unique essence or identity. Thus transformed, families are able to apply new patterns to life cycle tasks as they continue the journey.

4. Families are enlightened and empowered for their change

by the Holy Spirit. The transforming agent in the above story is the Wind, the dominant biblical image for the life-giving Spirit of God, Author of all change and growth. Family transformation occurs through letting go of human efforts to move forward and allowing the transcendent Spirit to carry the family to a new place. Letting go represents an intentional decision on the part of family members. It is thus through mobilizing their own inner intentionality that they raise their "vapor into the welcoming arms of the Wind."

5. Families are introduced into the Spirit's change process through the medium of words. The hidden voice of the desert utters words which open new possibility. The words that lead to family change are not ordinary words, however. They, like the words of this story, are of a special variety—metaphoric words.

I believe that these five principles are rich with potential for generating new approaches to family ministry. The rest of this book will be an unfolding of these principles and an application of them to family enrichment, education, and therapy.

Words ... Words ... Words ...

I want to unfold the fifth principle first for it opens upon and enlightens each of the other four. The essence of this principle is that families are transformed through metaphoric words.

Contemporary psychotherapy has developed a fascination with the power of words to evoke change. Cognitive behavior therapist Donald Meichenbaum has studied the effect of words which a person says to himself in maintaining self-defeating behavior and has learned that changing one's self-statements can lead to mood changes and actual behavioral change. Meichenbaum sums up his view by quoting Castaneda's Don Juan: "The world is such-and-such or so-and-so because we tell ourselves that that is the way it is . . . you talk to yourself. . . . We carry on internal talk. . . . In fact we maintain our world with our internal talk."*

Further understanding of this world-creating internal talk comes from those who have studied the work of Arizona psychiatrist and hypnotherapist Milton Erickson. Paul Watzlawick dedicates his recent book, *The Language of Change,* to "Dr. Milton H. Erickson Who Heals with Words."†

In this book Watzlawick refers to studies investigating the differing functions of the left and right hemispheres of the brain. The "left brain" performs rational, analytical functions and the "right brain" metaphorical, synthesizing, and holistic functions. As a result people communicate through two quite different languages: precise, logical left-brain expression and figurative, metaphorical right-brain talk. An example of left-brain communication would be: "The role expectations of married American males and females are changing today." An example of right-brain expression is Shakespeare's "All the world's a stage, and all the men and women merely players."

Watzlawick further states that an important function of the right brain is to synthesize each person's life experience into a holistic metaphor or "world image" unique to that person. The individual then uses that world image to interpret and make sense out of reality. The person perceives life through that image and responds to the world on the basis of perceptions colored by the image. For a person's responses to change requires changes in that person's world image. Since the world image is a right-brain creation, anyone seeking to facilitate change must communicate to the person in right-brain language, that is, in metaphoric words.

Family Metaphors

I believe that a family also has its own unique world images. Through its world images or metaphors a family interprets the world and responds to it. Family metaphors are created by the interaction of the world images of the two spouses who form the family. The resulting family metaphors give direction and meaning to the family's development and at times may also block its movement.

For example, early in life and long before they met one another John and Edna had both developed a similar world image belief that "we are people who lean on no one but achieve everything by our own hard work." When they met, married, and developed a family, this belief became a dominant metaphor in the family. A severe physical illness disabled John so that he was unable to work, and both he and Edna became acutely depressed, partly from lacking any social support network. In this crisis no amount of left-brain, rational advice to turn to others for help got through to John and Edna. But a series of metaphoric, right-brain messages—one of which was the story at the beginning of this chapter—led this family to create a new metaphor for themselves: "We can let go and receive help from God through other people." This new world image both opened up new ways to resolve the crisis and changed John and Edna's family.

Humanistic psychologist Bob Samples terms the right-brain functions the "metaphoric mind." I will use this descriptive term throughout the rest of the book for right-brain functioning. Samples writes thus about the creative activity of the metaphoric mind in changing world images: "When an idea comes into the metaphoric mind, a sudden rush of relationships flashes into being, and the original thought expands rapidly outward into a network of new holistic perceptions. The role of metaphoric thinking is to invent, to create, and to challenge conformity by extending what is known into new meadows of knowing."*

Samples adds that the functioning of the left brain, or "rational mind," is also important. The rational mind takes the world image created by the metaphoric mind and consolidates it through analysis, elaborates it through application to situations, and translates it into rational, explanatory language. Samples advocates respect for and use of both metaphoric and rational minds. The functioning of the two minds can be integrated as they work together in a harmonious partnership that can be termed the "synergic mind."†

Metaphoric Words and the Bible

The contemporary understanding of how the metaphoric mind is influenced through words can deepen our appreciation of how words are used in the Bible. The Bible is a book of metaphoric words. Throughout its pages we read imagistic, dreamlike language: "streams of living water," "valley of the shadow of death," "the wolf shall dwell with the lamb," "the sun of righteousness shall rise with healing in its wings," "the light shines in the darkness," "tongues as of fire," and "one like a son of man . . . his voice was like the sound of many waters." Jesus spoke of "bread from heaven" and "new wineskins" and used as his chief teaching medium the parable, a powerful vehicle for communicating with the metaphoric mind.

Metaphoric communication in the Bible comes not only by spoken words but also through visual experiences. While the "word of the Lord" came predominantly to biblical prophets and leaders in verbal form, it also frequently came in visions and dreams. We recall Jacob's dream of a ladder extending to heaven and Isaiah's awesome vision in the temple. Not only did the prophets "hear" God speaking to them, but we read frequently about the word of the Lord which the prophet "saw." Ezekiel saw "visions of God," including one of the Spirit breathing life into dry bones that filled a valley. At times the prophet is required to communicate through visible demonstration, as Hosea did in enacting a parable so that the people could see the message. John's Gospel highlights Jesus' communication through the "signs" of his miracles.

Words are more than verbal or visual expressions in the biblical world view, however. In its Near Eastern and Hebraic origins the concept of "word" in the Bible means also "thing," "action," and "event." Words have creative, dynamic power. God speaks and a thing comes into being: " 'Let there be light'; and there was light." The word that goes forth from God's mouth "shall not return to me empty, but it shall accomplish that which I purpose." Words are regarded as having healing power, as in Psalm 107:20: "He sent forth his word and healed them," or the healing expressions of Jesus: "Be cleansed," "Be opened," and "Young man, I say to you, arise." The culmination of the biblical idea of word as action or event, of course, occurred when "the Word became flesh" in Jesus.

Finally, the biblical word is often a word of command. Action is commanded. The Bible's language includes many imperatives, such as that to Abraham: "Go from your country . . . to the land that I will show you," and to Moses: "Lift up your rod, and stretch your hand over the sea and divide it." Familiar imperatives of Jesus include: "Follow me," "Feed my sheep," "Go and do likewise," and "Do this in remembrance of me."

Thus, in the Bible the metaphoric word comes in diverse forms, sometimes verbal, sometimes visual, sometimes action, and sometimes imperative. All of these forms are important to metaphoric communication, as we will see further in chapter 3.

More than Metaphor

While viewing the power of biblical language as words addressing the metaphoric mind, however, we must remember that its power is more than that of metaphor. Words as effectors of change are important only in light of principle 4 above, that change is empowered by the transcendent Wind, the Holy Spirit.

A description of Jesus' words in the Fourth Gospel is most helpful at this point: "It is the spirit that gives life, the flesh is of no avail; the words that I have spoken to you are spirit and life" (John 6:63). Here, as in the explanation to Nicodemus of how a person is transformed ("born again" and "born from above") by the mysterious action of the windlike Spirit (John 3:3–8), the point is that human beings cannot change themselves. Rather change is the creative act of the life-giving Spirit of God. The power of Jesus' words lay not merely in the fact that they spoke to the metaphoric mind of his listeners but more in the fact that they were words penetrated by the Spirit, the transcendent Source of life.

As we seek to minister creatively to families, I believe that we need to do so from a transcendent, spiritual perspective. Such a perspective reminds us that the power to transform lives comes from beyond ourselves. We can learn to use words with increased skill, but we are dependent creatures who need to rely upon a transcendent Wind to empower our human words. With Paul we say, "I planted, Apollos watered, but God gave the growth."

A transcendent, spiritual perspective also gives meaningful purpose and direction to our efforts at family change. In pastoral care change is not for the sake of change itself but for the increase of God-authored new and abundant life, which John Cobb describes as "wholeness centered in spirit."*

Words, Spirit, and Families

In unfolding the five principles with which I began I have now explained how families are transformed through metaphoric words—principle 5—and empowered by the Holy Spirit—principle 4. I want now to show more fully how that transformation occurs by further examining principles 1, 2, and 3.

Families in Transition

The first principle refers to time. Families are forever moving across time, journeying through the stages of the family life cycle. To understand the needs of a particular family, we need first to ask, What time is it for them? That is, What moment are they encountering in the family life cycle?

The *family life cycle* is a term employed in the literature of family sociology and family therapy to designate a fairly standard sequence of transitions through which most families go in the course of their life history. These transitions are brought on by the occurrence of a series of expectable events which change the composition of the family or the degree of member participation in the family, such as getting married, the birth of a child, children entering school, children leaving home, retirement, and death. Each transition thrusts upon the family a set of new tasks to perform. These tasks grow out of both the changing needs of the family's members and the changing expectations of the society outside the family that the family should accomplish certain tasks at particular times.

This combination of changing member needs and societal expectations impels the family forward through the life cycle, pushing it toward ever further development and differentiation. There is momentum and force to family growth through time.

Blocked Passages

The second principle states that families get blocked by applying old approaches to new life cycle passages. John and Edna's independence, useful earlier in their lives, blocked them at the time of crisis. Old approaches are patterns of thinking and interacting that families develop in order to put a check on the momentum of change impelling them through the life cycle. By developing these patterns, a family stabilizes itself and gives itself a sense of order, identity, and continuity in the face of change. So a second question we need to ask of a particular family we are serving is, What patterns are they using?

Like the rest of the natural world, the human family exists between relentless forces for change and persistent forces for stability. Stabilizing forces preserve the family from undergoing too rapid a change. Each family seeks to find its own balance between the change forces and the stability forces, a balance which both encourages development and promotes continuity.

The notion of balance grows out of the contemporary conception of the family as a "system," a dynamically organized grouping of members. The key to the idea of system is the human tendency to organize. People organize their ways of behaving with each other, including who does what to whom and who is primary and secondary in status or power. It is organization that gives the family system the holistic quality of being more than the sum of its parts, more than a collection of individuals.

By organizing itself a family achieves a dynamic balance between change forces and stability forces. An effective balance is one that provides sufficient structure to give the family the continuity and stability to survive while also providing its children sufficient flexibility to develop as individuals and leave the family at the appropriate time.

Each particular family organizes itself through creating its own unique metaphors or world images. As I have suggested above, a family's metaphors grow out of the world images of its founding partners and provide direction to the family's activity and development.

While family metaphors are created by the interaction of the metaphoric minds of its members, particularly of the parents, the implementing and rationalizing of the metaphors is effected by their left-brain, rational minds. This implementing and rationalizing result in verbal expressions of the metaphors, reality-defining statements like "We are a humble family" or "People can't be trusted." Implementing also results in behavioral expressions of the metaphors, repetitious sequences of acts among the members. Family members develop repetitive patterns of dealing with each other, such as son Bob acting up every time Mom and Dad are about to begin an argument. Families also develop hierarchical arrangements, such as Mom in charge of household operations with Dad second in command, while the situation is reversed with respect to the yard and garage, where Dad bears the primary responsibility and authority.

The implementing, rationalizing functions go on and on in the family in order to consolidate, reinforce, and maintain a metaphor that is vital to the family's functioning. If information contrary to the metaphor enters the family system, these rationalizing functions act to contradict the information or to incorporate it into a further refinement of the original metaphor.

Inevitably a situation will arise in the family's journey through the life cycle for which the old patterns are inadequate to meet the new tasks necessitated by changing member needs and societal expectations. Carefully supervising all of Bob's activity worked when he was only three but meets resistance at age thirteen. The family at this point often gets blocked by repetitively trying to force the old patterns on the new situation. Old wineskins don't work with new wine.

Transformation and Integration

The third principle I stated at the beginning of the chapter now comes into play. A family continues on its life cycle journey by finding a new way through the blocked passage. Family members initiate new patterns by altering the way they do things. John and Edna accept help from others, and Bob's parents permit him increased privacy and autonomy. So a third question that can be asked of a particular family is, What new patterns may they be evolving?

The new patterns that a family evolves strike a new balance in the family system. This new balance represents a creative integration of the change forces and the stability forces in the family.

Such an integration is the function of the metaphoric minds of the family members. Their metaphoric minds synthesize the old family metaphor and the new life cycle experience into a new holistic metaphor that both preserves the family's identity and enables its members to change.

This integrative process is a spiritual function in that it integrates by being transcendent of both the change-promoting and the pattern-maintaining forces. The activity of the transcendent Holy Spirit is needed because the human tendency is to fall in love with the attractiveness of change or power, or to grasp onto old patterns for the feelings of safety and comfort given by their familiarity. Either change/power or safety/comfort can become idolatrous, graven images. Families need to be empowered by the Holy Spirit, who criticizes all our human images and who authors new metaphors in light of the divine intention for our lives.

In creating new metaphors within families, the Spirit may speak to family members through interaction with other families or with lay and clergy facilitators. Metaphoric communication from these persons outside the family may be used by the Spirit to transform prevailing family metaphors into new ones. The new metaphors will aid the family in meeting God's direction for their lives through the tasks of the new family life cycle stage, but these metaphors in turn will also need to be transformed at subsequent stages of the life journey.

In this chapter I have begun to unfold five principles of family change. In the next chapter I will illustrate the interaction of these principles by describing the passage of one particular family through the life cycle. This will give opportunity to examine in more detail the specific tasks families face in the successive stages of the life-span, how families may get blocked, and how they get moving again. In chapter 3 I will specify some of the techniques of metaphoric communication that can facilitate family transformation at the passageways. In the remaining chapters I will apply these principles and techniques to three forms of family ministry: family enrichment, family life cycle education, and pastoral family therapy.

The journey beckons. Let us allow the Wind to carry us over the sand.

2. The Family Life Cycle

Anne, in the "Mary Worth" comic strip, says, "There comes a time in middle age when you take a good look at your life, Mary —and realize that if it is ever to be more meaningful you have to . . . to break the pattern!"*

In this chapter I will follow the course of one family's "breaking the pattern" as they proceed through the successive stages of the family life cycle. The story of this imaginary family represents a compilation of the experiences of a number of families that I have known at varying stages of their life cycles. I will use this family's story to illustrate the interaction of the five principles of this book over the life-span.

I will describe the course of the family life cycle as consisting of seven stages, beginning with disengagement from former family ties with a view to marriage and the establishment of a new family. As I do so I will not attempt to explore all of the tasks at each of the seven stages but refer the reader to more detailed descriptions available in the literature.† I also want to make no claim that the particular order of life stages I outline here applies to all families, for every family is unique and charts its own course. The family life cycle of a two-parent nuclear, Protestant, middle-class family described would need to be modified for families of other forms and socioeconomic conditions, as well as families whose life cycle has been interrupted by such events as divorce or death. Given these limitations, however, I suggest that this family's story parallels events experienced by many of the families in our churches.

Leaving Father and Mother

Bill and Jan met during their sophomore year at college. Both had come from religiously conservative, close-knit families. Going to a college several hundred miles away from each of their homes had been a difficult experience for them the previous year. Bill had felt homesick and almost phoned his parents the first weekend to ask for bus fare home. A roommate's invitation to an informal party started him on some small, tentative steps toward interacting with other students. In a few weeks he was beginning to form friendships with males and females, using some social skills he had begun to develop the last two years of high school.

Jan's progress was slower. She cried nightly for several weeks. She had not dated in high school, inhibited by her strict mother's spoken and unspoken messages that sexuality was dangerous and bad. Jan conceived of herself as a "good girl" except that she had some body parts that were "bad." Late in the fall Jan attended a retreat led by a campus pastor, who talked to the students about God intentionally creating us male and female and then declaring that our sexuality "was very good." As the pastor went on to discuss sexuality as "God's good gift to us," Jan experienced the dawning of a new awareness.

Conversations with the pastor and beginning dating experiences followed for Jan. She and Bill met the following year and were soon going with each other. Lack of extensive dating experience made for a confusing period of decision making for them, but they eventually decided to marry before their senior year.

Bill was surprised when his parents reacted negatively to this decision. Bill's father was adamant that Bill should postpone marriage until after graduation and a year or two of getting established in a job. Having viewed himself up to this time as a loyal son who pleased his parents, it was difficult for Bill to oppose their will. A period of much conversation with Jan and protracted wrestling in prayer eventuated in Bill coming to the realization that he could tell his parents that he appreciated their love and concern but that he must do what he and Jan felt led to do. Other loyalties beckoned him.

The first stage of the family life cycle involves a young person in the task of disengaging from the parental family and engaging in interaction with people one's own age. A variety of interpersonal skills must be learned, especially in the areas of forming outside-the-family friendships, courting the opposite sex, decision making, and verbal and sexual communication. When the young persons' families of origin are particularly tight-knit, as with Bill and Jan, this learning may be slowed or postponed.

Disengaging from one's previous family in order to start a new one can also be slowed by parental resistance to releasing their children. Unlike the mother bear who runs her cubs up a tree and abandons them, the human parent frequently encourages his or her offspring to remain longer in the original home. Leaving father and mother involves much more than physically leaving home for college or apartment. It involves emotionally disengaging from the parents without either running away in resentment or staying in conformity. While the task of leaving father and mother must be underway for people approaching marriageable age, this task is not quickly completed and continues to be worked on in succeeding stages of the life cycle.

The interaction of my five principles is apparent in the way Bill and Jan moved through this first passageway. The change momentum of new interpersonal tasks was blocked by patterns of thinking and acting based on metaphors regarding sexuality and family loyalty. The Holy Spirit acted through a pastor's image of "God's good gift" for Jan and through a realization of new levels of loyalty for Bill. These transforming experiences led to new metaphors that enabled Jan and Bill to move on.

Beginning to Build a Marriage

Bill and Jan were married the summer before their senior year, with both sets of parents in attendance. The bride and groom had a week-long honeymoon, full of pleasant discoveries of each other. Then came their first week back in their own off-campus apartment, full of some not so pleasant discoveries of each other.

Jan was reading one afternoon when Bill asked her to go out and play tennis with him. Jan declined, saying she wished to continue reading. Bill was immediately hurt and angry and insisted that she should *want* to go with him. Jan was surprised and angered by his harsh tone of voice, and the conversation ended in cold silence.

The next day Jan was preparing dinner when Bill entered the kitchen. He volunteered his help by beginning to show her how to prepare the vegetables for the salad. Bill was startled when Jan became upset and left the room enraged and crying, her voice quaking something about "keep out of my territory or I'll leave!"

Later that evening they talked. At first the mood of the conversation was stormy, each of them expressing some of their disappointments in the other. They then began to discuss what each wanted from the other and to work out some tentative agreements. At the end of the evening they felt closer to each other than they had ever before. Both had a vague idea that something important had happened.

As David and Vera Mace, pioneers in the marriage enrichment movement, often say, "A wedding is not a marriage!" By that they mean that the wedding is an event in which a couple publicly declares that they *intend* to build a marriage, a task that will take years of hard work to accomplish.

In the early phase of a marriage relationship couples are faced with a host of new tasks, many of them involving working out agreements about how they will relate to each other in the multiple facets of an intimate relationship. Gradually the partners form a number of expressed and unexpressed rules that define how the partners relate, and even rules that define how rules are to be made and carried out.

Metaphors and patterns defining what marriage is and how it should be lived have been internalized by the newly married partners through growing up exposed to the marriages of their parents. Since the marriages the partners have come from differ, the two people are soon involved in shaping new metaphors that incorporate both sets of expectations.

Bill and Jan were involved in defining their marriage relationship in such areas as who tells whom what to do, who has priority in what area, and how to deal with disagreements.

The last area, working out rules for handling disagreements, may be most important of all. Some couples form patterns of avoiding disagreeing openly and as a result accumulate underlying resentment, while others develop habits of chronic fighting that undermine each other's self-esteem. Still other couples discover with Bill and Jan that by talking through disagreements to mutual understanding they come to a greater closeness.

The press of these developmental tasks in this second phase of Bill and Jan's family life cycle collided with patterns from earlier times. Each had been raised as an only-child "princess" or "prince" in their families and expected that the other would continue to render them the homage to which they were accustomed. Now in this passageway they discovered that they both could not be "first in the kingdom"—or in the bathroom. Jan was raised by parents who avoided overt conflict, while Bill grew up observing parents disagree openly. The evening-long conversation represented the inbreaking of new metaphors: "shared royalty that can take turns getting our needs met" and "partners who can disagree and be close."

Giving Birth

In the second year of their marriage Bill and Jan welcomed the birth of their first child, Jerry. The couple, and Jan especially, plunged zealously into caring for the needs of this delightful—but demanding—little one. Bill sometimes chided himself for occasional feelings of irritation at Jan's giving so much more attention to Jerry. Two years later it was Jerry's turn to experience irritation when his parents brought home from the hospital a new little sister, Darlene.

It was the following year that Bill and Jan for the first time left the little ones over a weekend with Bill's parents as Bill and Jan attended a marriage enrichment retreat sponsored by their church. Two thoughts struck home that weekend. The hours spent talking alone with each other were like rain falling on a desert; they realized how little they had talked meaningfully with each other since the children were born. And the experience of sharing with other couples and being nurtured by them was even more of a revelation; they realized how hungry they were for supportive relationships outside their own little family. As they drove home that Sunday evening Bill and Jan committed themselves to some new directions for their relationship.

Many couples today wrestle with the decision whether or not to have children. Some postpone giving birth to children while both partners pursue career goals, while others decide not to have children at all. Still other couples, like Bill and Jan, elect to have children early in their marriage.

Partners who give birth to children find themselves facing a challenging set of new tasks. The birth of a first child changes the whole structure of a family. Rules that were worked out for two players now need to expand to include three. The demands for physical and emotional feeding of children put new demands upon the sources for the feeding of their parents. The focus upon parental roles frequently leads to the neglect of marital roles. Observers of young families note that young parents talk to each other about half as much as newlyweds and, when they do talk, talk more about their children than about themselves.

As young adults become caretakers of children the unanswered question frequently is, Who takes care of the adults?

Bill and Jan inherited from their families of origin a joint family metaphor of a close-knit, child-centered family that met its own needs. The demands of raising two small children close in age put pressure on behavioral patterns growing out of this metaphor that Bill and Jan were attempting to follow. Experiences at the retreat opened the possibility for new metaphors: "In order to give nurture we need to receive nurture from each other" and "We can belong to a nurturing community of other families!"

Letting My People Grow

A new turn came in the family's life one September morning when Jerry left for his first day of school. Jan felt a twinge of anxiety—her son was being influenced by people outside the family. But two Septembers later Jan felt even more of an impact when she came home from dropping Darlene off at school. She felt all alone in the house. In the ensuing weeks Jan grew increasingly depressed. A new problem soon occupied her attention as Jerry developed night terrors and a variety of daytime fears. Jan increased her involvement in his life, becoming his class's room mother, reading stories to him in the evening, and listening to his fears at length. Jerry's anxieties worsened. Jan suggested to Bill that perhaps Jerry needed counseling. At this point Bill, out of his own feelings of uncertainty and inadequacy to help, blew up and accused Jan of "making mountains out of molehills" with Jerry's problem. Jan was incensed. There followed the biggest fight of their marriage. When the debris had settled, Jan had decided to turn the care of Jerry's problem over to Bill and to do what she had been putting off, going back to school.

Only very gradually did matters improve in the family. However, two years later found Jerry mostly over his fears (largely due to being preoccupied with a new buddy who had moved into the neighborhood), Jan graduating in a master's program and taking a job, and the marriage somehow better for the wear and tear.

I have entitled this fourth stage in the family life cycle "letting my *people* grow" because the central task of this stage—family members developing individual identity outside the family—applies both to children and to their parents. Children need to form friendships with peers and learn from other adults. Fathers and mothers need also to develop such friendships and to prepare for an identity beyond childrearing. This task fell hardest on Jan, who had most heavily invested in parenting, but also bothered Bill, who by clinging to a belief in family self-sufficiency denied the need for outside help.

Once again developmental pressures challenged this family's propensity for returning to the metaphor of the close-knit, self-sufficient family. It was years later that Bill and Jan, looking back on this period of their lives, discerned the hand of the Spirit drawing all four members of their family into increased involvement in the world outside the family. Quietly over the years a new family metaphor had been evolving: "We are individuals, yet close."

Emancipating from Each Other

Jerry's experience of outside companionship expanded by the time he entered adolescence to include additional buddies, and he had developed a gang of close friends. He spent more and more time with his peers and less with his parents. When he was at home he holed up in his room with his stereo. When Jerry was thirteen Jan had a series of dreams about animals dying, and one in which Jerry died. She sensed intuitively from this that her son was gradually leaving her emotionally, and she was accepting it. She also confirmed Darlene's separating from her. Learning from her life experience with her own mother, Jan encouraged Darlene to date and took pride in her emerging beauty as an exceptionally attractive teenager. Darlene gained from close talks with Jan about sexuality, but at times she chose not to talk with her Mom about what she was doing or thinking.

Bill shared Jan's pride and enjoyment in their two children and remarked to her that the kids were fast becoming their friends instead of their children.

But one incident revealed that Bill was having some difficulty with his relationship to his son. Jerry announced during his junior year that he planned to spend his savings from part-time jobs to buy a used car. Bill opposed his choice of car, and the two were soon in a heated argument. Through the conversation Bill discovered that he opposed Jerry's decision not only because he thought the car in question was defective but also because he had not really accepted Jerry's decision not to go on to college; he still hoped Jerry would change his mind about higher education and have the needed savings on hand when he did. Jerry told his dad to stop trying to run his life. He bought the car, and it did turn out to be a bad choice. Afterward Jerry appreciated his dad not saying "I told you so," and Bill had the feeling that both of them had grown up through this experience.

The central task of this fifth stage of family life is for parents and their teenage children to achieve emancipation from each other. Parents facilitate this process by gradually allowing their relationship with their children to shift; instead of treating them as dependent children they begin to relate to them as autonomous adults. "Wise parents guide their adolescents with a loose rein, letting them have their heads, knowing that they will not stray too far from the fold if they are not driven from it."*

Teens facilitate this process by investing in peer relationships while not provoking their parents through either overdependency or overrebelliousness.

Bill and Jan and their children generally encouraged this process reciprocally. However, Bill and Jan at times seized upon the age-old wish to be able to take the adults' accumulation of wisdom gained from life experience and hand it over to youth so that youth won't have to go through the pain and make the same mistakes their parents did. As a friend of mine says, "This is a very nice idea. The only problem is, in human history it hasn't yet worked!" Bill learned about that through the car purchase incident.

This latter incident again reveals the changes of developmental time pressing upon past patterns, in this case Jerry's need to make decisions of his own and Bill's need to protect his son from the hurt of mistakes. In the eventual outcome the two males came out with a transcendent result—a relationship of mutual respect.

Letting People Go

Jerry moved out of the house when he got his first full-time job after high school graduation. Bill and Jan had a sense of satisfaction as they helped him move into his small apartment. Darlene's departure was more trying: she moved in with her boyfriend. Bill and Jan talked long with her and with each other, wrestling with the issue of whether they could accept her differing values. Following her leaving Bill and Jan found themselves dealing with another issue: they were alone together in the house. "It's like we don't seem to have anything to say to each other," Bill confided to his best friend in the church. The friend suggested what he and his wife had done at this same time, taking a second honeymoon trip. Shortly thereafter Bill and Jan took that trip and experienced a deepened intimacy. Upon their return they told friends, "We have rediscovered each other."

Jay Haley labels this sixth stage of the family life cycle "weaning parents from children" to underscore its central task: parents releasing their young adult children to live lives of their own. If parents have not cultivated their marriage relationship during the years that they have been heavily involved rearing children, they may have difficulty letting these children be apart without seeking to remain involved in their lives. The departure of the last child particularly brings the need for parents to renew their marriage. They may discover a new joy as they begin the second half of the time-span of marriage alone together, the way they began more than two decades ago.

On the other side of the "launching center" family stand the young adults with their need to separate physically from the parents while staying in positive emotional relationship with them. Sometimes young adults abort this process by staying at home under parental control or by leaving home in hostile rebellion. Both of these reactions prevent emotional disengagement.

Bill and Jan, feeling the press of the changed situation of the empty nest against the pattern of their close involvement with their children, were facilitated by a friend's advice toward a new level of integration, a renewed marriage.

Retiring and Letting Go

Jan retired from her job about five years prior to Bill's retirement and became increasingly involved with her church and with Maureen, a widowed friend. At Bill's retirement the couple enjoyed a long-contemplated trip and then settled back into their home. In the days that followed Bill felt hurt that Jan resumed her former pace of activity with church and with Maureen, frequently leaving him at home alone when he felt so much need for her companionship. When he expressed this frustration one day, Jan replied with her frustration at his constantly being in her way around the house and disrupting her household routines. Drawing upon skills first developed in confrontation after the honeymoon more than four decades before, Bill and Jan worked out some new agreements.

The death of Bill's best friend from church, followed within a month by Maureen's death, shook Bill and Jan deeply. Each succeeding loss brought them face to face with long-ignored realities approaching in their own life-span: the day of the death of their spouse and the final day of their own life. Bill and Jan were silent during their church's study group session on death one Sunday morning, but in the car on the way home they initiated a most significant conversation. Through it they reconfirmed and extended a metaphoric theme that had been developing through all their family history: a willingness to let go of everything—including family—while being raised into the wider family of God.

This theme sustained Jan through the valley of deep grief she entered when Bill died six months later. In the years that followed Jan learned new skills of painting and piano playing that contributed to her own enjoyment and that of her family and friends. When asked about how she was coping with Bill's loss she would reply, "I miss him terribly. I think that the hole will always be there. But I am learning that my life can still be rich, and I feel closer to others and to God than ever before."

Retirement often brings the welcome opportunity of an abundance of free time and the unwelcome realization that spending twenty-four hours a day with one's spouse can be a mixed blessing. The needs a husband was meeting through work relationships are now placed upon the marriage relationship. Developing new friendships and activities outside the marriage is often vital at this time to complement the search for intimacy within the marriage.

Aging persons are faced with the challenge of coping with losses in many areas of life: social, financial, physical, and in self-esteem. But here again the Spirit "helps us in our weakness," enabling family members to let go of loved ones in a renewal of faith.

Through the course of a long marriage Bill and Jan had formed a deep attachment to each other, the powerful bonding that is the nature of marriage. The life cycle events of retirement and the death of one's spouse brought major challenges to their investment in that attachment. However, their metaphoric minds integrated the image of that attachment with a new, holistic metaphor of a yet deeper bonding, their participation in the family of God. At the end of the life cycle journey they prepared themselves to let go of life itself, crossing the last desert by allowing themselves to be raised into the arms of the welcoming Wind.

3. Techniques of Metaphoric Communication

Mary was discouraged. Sitting across from Pastor Evans in his office, she described her forty-eight years of life as having left her frustrated and tired, a "rat race going nowhere." She suffered from daily headaches, being overweight and feeling generally depressed and listless. She had difficulty getting out of bed each morning to begin the day. What made her most unhappy was her twenty-eight-year marriage to Ed. She complained that Ed didn't share his feelings with her, leaving her feeling empty and alone. She could not see leaving Ed, however, for she guessed that would only increase her loneliness. She had "sacrificed" herself for Ed and the three children they had raised and now felt worn out. The youngest child, a daughter, Sandy, had a chronic illness. Sandy had moved out of the house to an apartment two years ago, relieving some of the pressure on Mary. However, Sandy still visited the home a lot, and Mary feared that in the future Sandy's condition would worsen and "I will wind up taking care of her."

Mary told Pastor Evans that she hadn't wanted to come to see him because she realized that "effort" would be required to solve the problem and she did not feel she could handle any more stress. Pastor Evans replied, "Sometimes when we give up, the solution comes effortlessly." He then asked her to have Ed call him for an appointment.

Ed did come to see Pastor Evans and expressed his long-standing concern for Mary's "unhappiness." He said that he knew he was poor at communicating feelings, but he believed his wife's problem was her own and a deep-seated one. He was glad she was talking to Pastor Evans and agreed to come in with her at a later date if that would be helpful.

Mary came back to see Pastor Evans for several more meetings. On one occasion she began by describing herself as feeling burdened. Pastor Evans asked her to close her eyes, relax, and describe literally the burden that she was feeling. She did so and said there was a "burden of guilt on my shoulders . . . weighing me down." Pastor Evans asked her to examine the burden in detail and describe it. Mary replied that it resembled "a heavy old man riding on my shoulders and driving me." Pastor Evans asked Mary what she wanted to do with the burden. "Throw it off." Pastor Evans directed Mary to imagine in detail removing this burden from her back. Mary at once burst into tears. When the pastor inquired about that, Mary replied, "I can't throw him off because he will just pursue me and climb back on, and I will feel even worse." Pastor Evans suggested that in her imagination she could come up with a solution that could keep "him" off permanently. Mary then visualized throwing the man off, and the man was standing along the roadway behind her as if looking to get back on. Suddenly there came into her mind the image of a plate of armor appearing on her shoulders, with long, sharp points protruding upward. The man turned away from her, afraid to try to mount that foreboding armament. Mary was elated at that and discovered to her further delight that the armor was "amazingly light" so that she didn't even feel it on her shoulders! As she continued to imagine, she felt "light, so light I am floating over the trees."

Pastor Evans instructed her to practice this image daily at home. He had earlier taught her to relax deeply and repeat to herself the affirmative thought, "I am learning to picture myself the way I want to be." He asked her now to visualize her new image in conjunction with that thought. He further suggested she might either express her experience in descriptive writing or in a drawing.

The next week Mary reported to Pastor Evans that she felt "born again." She described this as feeling "free and joyful."

"The burden is lifted," and "I am managing myself" instead of being controlled by others or by unpleasant feelings or circumstances.

Pastor Evans asked her to relate this experience to her religious understandings. Mary was unable to do so. She described her childhood religious training as being concerned with rules and guilt and teaching that one was to sacrifice oneself in this life in order to be happy in heaven. Pastor Evans reminded her that Jesus contrasted his religion to that of the Pharisees by saying the words, "For my yoke is easy, and my burden is light." Pastor Evans went on to relate a series of biblical stories of Jesus' interaction with people, including the conversation with Nicodemus at night and Jesus' visit to Mary and Martha that closed with him saying, "Martha, Martha, you are troubled about many things. One thing is needful."

A few weeks later Mary felt ready to have Ed join her in the sessions for marriage counseling. Ed, encouraged by her progress, was interested in working at the improvement of their relationship. Mary and Ed chose to focus on developing their communication. When Ed restated his belief that "I am a poor communicator" Pastor Evans responded that he had once heard someone say that "poor communicators are often good communicators who are lacking *practice.*"

Pastor Evans asked them to recall a time when they had a very positive experience of verbal sharing. Ed described a recent dinner at a restaurant when both of them were in what they termed a companionable mood. The pastor asked each of them for a detailed description of how that occurred, what each felt at the time, and what they noticed in each other. An animated conversation followed. Pastor Evans told Mary and Ed that both of them were now in a companionable part of themselves and suggested that they could do that spontaneously at home. Over the next weeks he assigned them various homework exercises involving their companionable parts, such as evenings out.

An important setback occurred a few weeks later. One morning Mary had been practicing her "light armor" imagery with intensity when her daughter, Sandy, dropped in unexpectedly to to use Mary's sewing machine and to visit for the day. Mary felt her mood destroyed and became depressed, at the same time feeling guilty about not wanting Sandy in her house. When Mary related this to Pastor Evans he instructed her to work out an arrangement with Sandy in which Sandy was to phone before she came to the house to use any of the appliances and that would allow Mary to be away from the house at those times if she desired. Any of Sandy's financial matters were to be discussed solely between Sandy and Ed.

Mary did this and felt relieved. The day of the next session Sandy phoned to ask if she could come over to use the sewing machine. Mary said not today but she could come over tomorrow while Mary was to be away at a luncheon.

A few weeks later Ed reported that the night before he had been disturbed by a series of vivid dreams. The last dream had been particularly frightening. In it their house had burned, and he and Mary were standing outside looking at its charred ruins. He described feelings of horror and despair. He awoke in a panic, sat up, and reached to see if Mary were still there. "I was afraid something had happened to her and she was gone."

Pastor Evans asked Ed to close his eyes and continue the dream by imagining that Ed himself was the house. Ed described feeling a lot of physical pain and then feeling burned and blackened. "I am all used up," he said. The remains of the house were then knocked down and carried away, and a new house was built on the same spot. Pastor Evans asked Ed to become the new house as it was being built and to continue on in the dream. Ed described a feeling of joy as the house was constructed. When the pastor asked Ed if there was anything more he wanted to do to complete the house, Ed imagined Mary coming up to the house, entering it, and moving in. She appeared excited and was laughing happily as she walked through the rooms.

Pastor Evans noticed Mary weeping during this last description. When he asked her a few moments later what had affected her, she replied, "He *wanted* me to live in his house!" She concluded that "Ed actually loves me!"

This is an account of an actual series of counseling sessions that occurred between a pastor and a couple at the "letting people go" stage of the family life cycle. Pastor Evans makes use of several techniques of metaphoric communication. In the rest of this chapter I will identify and explain eight of these techniques.

In chapter 1 I pointed out that the change activity of the Spirit operates through special words which address the metaphoric mind, enabling this part of the brain to transform previous word images or metaphors into new ones. I noted that these special words or metaphoric communication can take a variety of forms that reflect the multiple dimensions of the biblical conception of "word." Specifically these dimensions include imagistic, metaphorical words; visual experiences; actions or events; and imperatives. Eight techniques that reflect these varied dimensions are: active imagination, story/parable/dream, reframing, special language patterns, creative memory, action imperatives, affirmations, and play.

Active Imagination

When Pastor Evans asked Mary to close her eyes and imagine in detail removing the burden from her back, he was employing a visual form of metaphoric mind communication known as active imagination. This technique first involves selecting either an imagistic word that a person uses to describe a problem or an image that emerges from the report of a dream, such as Ed's burned house. The word or image is chosen because it is particularly vivid or meaningful to the person and is frequently repeated, or seems to the listener to summarize in a metaphor the difficulty being assessed or described. It is essential that the word or image chosen be that of the parishioner or client, not one proposed by the pastor or listener, in order for it to be addressed directly to the particular world image that they are seeking to change.

The pastor then asks the parishioner to close the eyes, as it is usually easier to visualize without outer visual distractions. Persons' inner concentration can be increased by having them relax thoroughly at this time, using any procedure for relaxation that they have learned. If they lack a means for relaxing, the pastor can teach them one, such as progressive relaxation.*

Next the pastor asks the person to imagine a picture of the

selected word and visualize this image in detail. Follow-up questions may be used to encourage detailed exploration, such as, "What exactly does it look like?" or "What color is it?"

Then the pastor asks the person to imagine the image changing in some way. It is important in this connection that the pastor *not* specify what kind of change is meant. Instead the pastor's request may vaguely suggest only that some action is possible, thereby allowing the metaphoric mind of the parishioner to fill in the details according to his or her own need. For example, Pastor Evans asked Mary what she wanted to do with the burden.

In the course of the subsequent interaction with the image, the parishioner may get blocked and need the encouragement of further vague suggestions from the pastor. When Mary feared that the burden would just climb back on her, Pastor Evans suggested she could imagine a permanent solution.

Finally, the pastor may facilitate the parishioner's integration of the experience by assigning the practice of visualizing it at home and expressing it in such forms as creative writing, poetry, or art, depending on the person's preferred mode of expression.

Pastoral counselor John Sanford, who traces the origin of the active imagination technique to Carl Jung, emphasizes the active dimension of this tool. Sanford stresses that the technique requires the parishioner or client to become an active participant dynamically involved with his or her own inner processes rather than a passive observer of them. This is hard work. Instead of doing the work *for* them the pastor firmly encourages parishioners to keep doing the work themselves. "People are lazy about their own psyches. We do not want to have to work on ourselves . . . [but] the fact is that we get well in direct proportion to the energy we put into our psychological development."*

The effectiveness of this technique lies not only in its active involvement of the parishioner but also in its employing the process of visualization, a function of the metaphoric mind. When persons begin to create pictures inside the mind, control is automatically shifted in that moment from the rational mind to the metaphoric mind.†

However, in addition to visual imagination, auditory, olfactory, feeling, and proprioceptive fantasy can be employed.* An excellent example of the use of all these dimensions is described by Bandler and Grinder, who use the term *guided fantasy* for this technique. They report that a woman expressed to them in a seminar that she felt she was going crazy in the face of an unknown and frightening future.

> The teacher of the seminar asked her to close her eyes and tell him what she saw. After some initial difficulty she proceeded to describe herself as standing on the edge of a large crevasse which was steep and foreboding. The teacher told her to slowly proceed into the crevasse ’and explore it, asking her to continually report on what she experienced, giving details of sight, hearing, feeling, smelling, and constantly reassuring her she could proceed through each obstacle. She finally proceeded down and back up, remarking when she arrived at the top again that it was still a gloomy day but that somehow she felt better. When she opened her eyes her fear was gone and she felt that she could survive all that faced her.†

Story/Parable/Dream

When Pastor Evans told Mary some stories from the Bible about Jesus interacting with Nicodemus and with Martha, and when he encouraged Ed to tell his dream, the pastor was utilizing a very ancient form of metaphoric communication, the story. The Bible itself is perhaps the best example of communicating truths through the form of stories and parables.

The figurative language of stories has the unique power of communicating multiple dimensions of meaning and influence all at once. Carl Fellner, who advocates the use of "teaching stories" for counseling families, states that this technique is particularly potent for influencing families because of the nature of the family as a system of multiple, interacting, mutually influencing factors. When a person has told a family such a teaching story, Fellner writes, "He has commented indirectly on several levels of meaning about an ongoing situation, and he has seeded a number of ideas, set in motion a number of forces. It is now up to the individuals themselves to make their own discoveries, their own interpretations, and thus move toward possibly perceiving relationships in new ways, toward 'tasting' new realities."‡

For example, telling the story of the stream and the desert at the beginning of this book could speak to family members on such diverse levels as their relationships with each other and with the pastor, their early memories of loving human touch through being held as infants, human weakness and limitations and transcendent divine intervention in human life, and many others.

A key reason for the effectiveness of stories is that the listener hears someone else or some other thing referred to in the story, with no direct reference to himself. It is the nature of our metaphoric mind to take such a vague, unrelated item and translate it into relevance for ourselves or our own situation.* Those who have studied Milton Erickson's work closely note his frequent use of such expressions as "A family came to me who . . ." or "I knew a woman once who . . .", expressions that allow listeners to fill in their own name. Hearing how other persons and families have made it through a life passage opens up possibilities for imagining how we might also. In the same way, you and I can relate the experience of the stream in the story above to our own life. In this way we experience the story for ourselves.

In selecting stories to tell a family in counseling, or a group of families in an educational event, a pastor first considers what family life cycle passage they are struggling to master. The stories chosen should reflect the painful dilemma the family is experiencing and also point toward a generalized resolution. A variation is to tell one or more stories that describe the dilemma, followed by a concluding story which suggests a way someone has resolved a similar problem. Families struggling with letting go of their children might, for example, be reminded of the parable of the prodigal son.

It is also helpful if the stories chosen can reflect the family's unique ways of expressing their own dilemma; a story can even be adapted to fit their exact words. After hearing Mary talk at length about "effort," "work," and "burden" Pastor Evans told her stories about hardworking Martha and Jesus' easy yoke and light burden. New stories can be created to fit specific needs of a particular family, as I will describe in chapter 6.

All of what I have said about stories applies equally to dreams, which convey our own life stories. The pastor can do more than simply encourage families to share their dreams; counselors can actually relate their own dreams, thereby sharing from their own life stories. Having family members relate and then extend their dreams in the presence of each other can be a powerful experience, as when Mary listened to Ed's dream of welcoming her into his new house.

Sanford suggests the use of prayer in connection with dreams. "If there is a dream figure who needs help—a retarded child perhaps, or an injured man or forlorn woman—we can pray for the dream figure just as we might pray for an outer person who is in difficulty."*

The activity of the Holy Spirit through stories and dreams is underscored by Sanford, who views the dream as God speaking to the whole community, the church. Dreams don't belong only to the dreamer; they belong to everyone. The Spirit sends nourishment for the whole community through his nightly metaphoric communication in the dreams of the community's members. Sanford adds, "Dreams may be the most frequent and important way in which the word of God is spoken."†

In addition to telling and using active imagination with stories and dreams, family members can enact or dramatize a story or dream. The pastor can instruct the members to perform together all the actions of the characters in, for example, the dream story of one of their members. Enactment has the advantage of involving all of our sensory modalities at once as we see, hear, and experience the drama.‡ Again, this use of metaphoric communication reminds us of the enacted parables of the Old Testament prophets.

Reframing

Mary expected that effort would be required to solve her problem. She viewed her problem and its solving within the framework of her metaphor or picture of the world—that endeavors in life required effort, sacrifice, and much giving. Mary as much as said so when she stated that she didn't feel she could exert any more effort. "Sometimes when we give up, the solution comes effortlessly" was Pastor Evans's response. His remark was puzzling to Mary. It caught her up short. Pastor Evans was suggesting that a solution to her problem might lie altogether outside of her assumed framework of effort and trying. This is reframing, a shifting of the way a problem is approached so that it is viewed from an entirely different perspective.

Reframing involves attributing to a situation a different meaning than the one a person is currently giving that situation. When I complain to my wife about all the work I have to do she reframes my situation by replying, "Aren't you fortunate to have so many interesting things to do!" Thus a previously unwanted experience can be redefined as potentially valuable.

Watzlawick has written extensively about this technique.* When people make an assumption about the way things *are* and that becomes the frame within which they look for solutions, they thereby create for themselves a problem. Limiting their thinking to this one frame blinds them to the possibility that there may be other solutions outside the frame. Reframing calls in question the very assumption underlying the person's frame and thus often sounds puzzling, illogical, and paradoxical to the hearer's rational mind. However, to the metaphoric mind it offers a new possibility by transcending the limits of the former frame. Suddenly the person views the problem in a new light.

At the base of Ed's frame was the assumption that there are poor communicators and he was born one. The only two choices available within this frame for Ed were either try to communicate and fail or not try and stay a poor communicator. Pastor Evans reframed this idea by his paradoxical remark that poor communicators are often good communicators who are lacking practice. By this remark Pastor Evans questioned Ed's basic assumption and opened the possibility that Ed could communicate. Similarly Pastor Evans reframed Mary's concept of religion as a heavy burden of rules to be obeyed and sacrifices to be made when he referred to Jesus' paradoxical description of his religion as a yoke that is easy.

Jesus' whole ministry on earth was itself a radical reframing of our human expectation. Instead of seeking to win our allegiance by a "winning" approach of dazzling us with attractiveness and conquering might, he lived and died an apparent "loser," "despised and rejected by men" and dying on a criminal's cross. But by losing he was victorious; he won our hearts. His paradoxical words are still relevant: "He who seeks to save his life will lose it, but he who loses his life for my sake will find it." These very words can profitably be spoken to family groups, for many a parent and child in our churches' families are seeking to "win" their point or to "win" respect in relationships.

Special Language Patterns

When Pastor Evans quoted to Mary from Jesus' words to Martha "one thing is needful" and responded to Ed that he had once heard someone say that "poor communicators are often good communicators who are lacking *practice*," he was using some special patterns of language particularly effective for communication to the metaphoric mind.

One of these is the aphorism, a short, pointed statement that concisely expresses a truth. Part of the impact of an aphorism lies in its combining two or more concepts into a startling association. The title of a recent book about loss and grief captures succinctly a truth for this life cycle experience, *When Going to Pieces Holds You Together.**

Pastor Evans's quotation of Jesus' words "my burden is light" is another aphoristic expression. Watzlawick writes: "It seems that there is something in the essence of a well-constructed aphorism that lends itself to an almost flashlike illumination of complex human situations and, therefore, also of world images."† Watzlawick goes on to list several other language forms that have similar effects, including condensations, puns, ambiguities, jokes, homonyms, and allusions.

A quotation itself is a special language pattern. An effect of quoting wise statements from someone else is that it enables the communicator to give a message or command directly to the metaphoric mind without the rational mind resisting and arguing with the communicator, since he was not the originator of the statement. Bandler and Grinder, who have studied these language patterns extensively, state that giving commands within quotations allows the metaphoric mind to actively participate in the interaction with the speaker and to choose to what portions of the speaker's communication to respond.* The effectiveness of these patterns is increased by "marking" or emphasizing different portions of a statement by pausing, by shifting tone, or by a gesture or shift of body posture. Marking has the same effect as emphasizing a word or phrase in written communication by underlining it or putting it in italics. When Pastor Evans verbally stressed the last word of his quotation to Ed, "Poor communicators are often good communicators who are lacking *practice,*" he was directing the last word as a command to Ed's metaphoric mind.

Another special language pattern that stimulates the metaphoric mind to participate actively is the use of nonreferring words and phrases. Ordinarily in speaking we try to choose words that refer specifically to the persons, actions, or experiences we wish the listener to understand from our communication. When we do the opposite and purposefully speak nouns and verbs that are nonspecific the metaphoric minds of our listeners go to work to translate those generalized words into the persons, actions, or experiences that best fit the listeners' own needs and goals. This gives listeners maximum freedom to choose the interpretation of the speaker's words that is most relevant for their life situation.

For example, a very specific sentence addressed to Mary, "Ed bought Mary a gift of a dozen red roses," could be rephrased: "Someone did something very meaningful for you on a certain occasion." The latter, generalized phrasing would allow Mary to recall a particular event that most fit her needs in that moment. Similarly a speaker can allow listeners to choose a future action or goal for themselves by phrasing a sentence vaguely, such as Pastor Evans's quotation to Mary, "One thing is needful." Mary's metaphoric mind then needed to act upon that communication to interpret what action she needed to perform to accomplish what goals.

Creative Memory

When Pastor Evans led Ed and Mary into a conversation that involved both their companionable parts, he was not creating something new that had not existed within these two people but rather facilitating the expression of these existing resources within them to change their relationship. Creative memory involves drawing upon and reshaping latent resources within families. Instead of a creation "out of nothing" it is a creation out of something.

The something out of which the creation is shaped is past experience. Bandler and Grinder view as a central assumption of Milton Erickson's work that persons who come for assistance of any kind already have within them the resources they need to accomplish their goals and make the changes they desire.*

These resources, they add, come from persons' life experiences, for all people have had experiences in which they displayed capacities for accomplishing the very changes they presently desire. These past experiences are stored and organized in the metaphoric mind. Words are attached to these organizations of experience and serve as labels for them, for example, "companionable," "happy," "confident," or "loving." When those labels are spoken in the present, the stored organization of past experience can be recalled.

When members of a family state a goal they desire, such as "to be loving," the pastor needs to ask them what the experience would be like if that goal were achieved. He may then ask them for a name for that experience or for names for the part of each person that would be acting in that experience, such as "loving friends." The pastor can then ask the family members to describe in detail one or more instances in which that experience occurred. The members, for example, may recall "loving" experiences. Pastor Evans requested Ed and Mary to describe a "companionable" experience.

As the family members are describing both the desired future and remembered past experiences, they are automatically utilizing their own internal resources for creating that experience right in the present moment. As this happens the family members have an experience of each other that can cause them to view each other differently. This experience can then become a springboard for further change and can be recalled by repeating the name attributed to the experience by the family.

Action Imperatives

The instructions Pastor Evans gave to Mary to arrange to be out of the house when her daughter visited led Mary to an experience of "relief." These and other homework assignments Pastor Evans gave to Ed and Mary resemble biblical language that takes the form of words of command or imperatives in that such instructions require people to actually *do* something different in their lives.

Giving persons a directive to do something different can lead to a change of their world images or metaphors. The very thought of carrying out the instruction, let alone the actual doing of it, brings into the persons' metaphoric minds a new experience that cannot be included in their old world image without changing that image.* To perform the requested actions necessitates persons drawing upon latent resources within themselves, thus discovering other parts of themselves. Asking Mary to say no to her daughter challenged the basic assumption of her world image that she was always to be a care giver who sacrificed her own needs to meet others' needs. When she carried out the pastor's instruction she had a new experience that at least partially changed her metaphoric-mind world image. She also discovered that she had a part of herself that felt very good about meeting her own needs.

The image-challenging nature of an action imperative can best be seen in Jesus' directives to people he met. Particularly interesting is his directing an injunction to the precise center of the rich young ruler's world image: "You lack one thing; go, sell what you have and give to the poor, . . . and come, follow me."

The action requested in an imperative need only be a very small, apparently insignificant one, however. This stems from another principle of the functioning of the metaphoric mind that Watzlawick terms *pars pro toto,* that is, a part stands for the whole.† The repeating of one small part of an experience leads the metaphoric mind to recall the whole experience. A line from a song brings to mind an entire movie. Similarly, asking a person to do one small thing related to the problem area—instead of trying to solve the entire problem all at once—may eventually generalize to even larger changes within that person's life or that family's interaction. Pastor Evans's instructing Ed to be the one handling financial matters with Sandy led to Ed's increased involvement—and Mary's decreased involvement—with Sandy.

Affirmations *

"I am learning to picture myself the way I want to be," the sentence Pastor Evans asked Mary to repeat to herself, is an example of an affirmation, or positive, personal expression.

In chapter 1 I referred to contemporary psychologists' study of the effect on our feelings and actions of the words we all say to ourselves, our private internal talk. If we would listen to the ongoing stream of messages we speak to ourselves about ourselves we would be surprised at how negative, unrealistic, and self-defeating the words may be. Replacing this negative record with a positive one can have a dramatic effect on one's feeling tone and behavior. One of the most powerful experiences of my own life occurred when a professor of mine suggested that I have a long inner dialogue with the part of myself that I most despised, the lazy, mistake-prone, failing side. In the dialogue I was to say all the things that I loved and valued about this part of me, appreciating it for what it had done for me. In the course of that inner dialogue I felt a sudden surge of tremendous joy and a deep sense of wholeness that comes from an experience of self-acceptance and self-affirmation.

Goals for personal growth can also be stated as affirmations and directed toward the metaphoric mind. It is important that such goal statements be worded positively. The metaphoric mind does not distinguish negations, such as "not" or "never." Phrasing a goal negatively, such as "I will not be shy and not stammer," points the metaphoric mind toward the personal goal of being shy and stammering. The best form is a positive "I am learning to . . ." beginning phrase followed by a succinct statement of a goal, such as ". . . to speak freely and with confidence." The effectiveness of the affirmation is increased by repeating it many times while visualizing a detailed image of yourself doing the goal behavior.

Affirmations are also very important communications between family members. They build the self-worth of the members and strengthen relationships. One of the most powerful growth experiences a family can have is to have its members take turns telling each other all the things they love, value, and appreciate about each other.

Play

After Mary's experience in the session in which she created the image of the "amazingly light armor," Pastor Evans suggested that she continue to express the image through writing and drawing. These activities are only a small example of this most varied technique area, creative play.

Actually all of the techniques described above could be called creative play, but in this eighth category I am thinking more specifically about those childlike activities that are engaged in for their own sake or at least for no other purpose than sheer fun.

Children learn most rapidly through their carefree play. When adults engage in childlike play, they discover that their metaphoric minds are stimulated and their powers of imagination unleashed. Their metaphoric minds begin to learn very rapidly, as they did in childhood.

In family educational events it is fascinating to watch adults and children play together such simple childhood games as "Mother May I?" and "Drop the Handkerchief" or active physical games such as volleyball that energize by stimulating the integration of body, mind, and spirit.

The imagination is also stirred by playful expression in such creative activities as fingerpainting, drawing, clay sculpting, dramatizing, writing poetry, and listening or dancing to music.

The eight techniques which I have described in this chapter can be used singly or in varied combinations to effect change in family members' metaphoric world images. All eight of them have in common the capacity for stimulating these changes through directly addressing the metaphoric mind. In the chapters ahead I will show how these techniques can be used in family enrichment, education, and therapy.

4. Marriage and Family Enrichment Programs

I will always remember an incident from one of my first family enrichment experiences. It occurred during an exercise at a family weekend program led by Russell Wilson at a state park near Nashville, Tennessee. I was seated facing my six-year-old son during an exercise in which each family member took turns expressing directly to other family members all the things that he or she most loves and values about them. I was surprised to discover all the loving, positive things I felt toward my son as I related them to him. When I finished, my son was asked to respond with only what he was feeling at the moment. He spontaneously jumped from his chair with a big smile, hugged me tightly, and said simply, "Daddy, I feel happy!"

Needless to say, my wife, Joan, and I felt very happy at that moment too! I later expressed to Joan that this event felt like rain falling upon parched earth, that the outpouring of loving, valuing statements seemed so much in contrast to the usual flow of corrective and negative remarks we address to the children in everyday living. Joan and I concluded that in this event we had tapped into a vast reservoir of potential within our family for increased caring, positive feelings, and spontaneous happiness and joy.

The marriage and family enrichment movement is based upon this very premise, that every couple and family have untapped potential for loving, caring, creativity, and joy that can be released through structured group experiences.* One type of these experiences is marriage enrichment, a program involving a group of married couples who meet together over a weekend or for a series of weekly meetings in which the primary focus is upon releasing the potential for positive interaction within the husband-wife dyad. Another program form is family enrichment, an experience in which a group of entire families meets together over a weekend or in a series of weekly meetings, forming together a supportive network to undergird participating families and to encourage each family to develop its unique strengths.

Principles of Family Transformation

Both of these enrichment forms draw upon the five principles of family transformation that I discussed in chapter 1.

First, banking upon the principle that marriages and families are dynamic entities—always moving, changing, and developing —enrichment programs are designed to invoke family capacities for change and growth present at all stages of the life cycle. Leaders of enrichment programs, because they are sensitive to the fact that marriages and families are not static but dynamic, communicate an expectant belief that each couple or family unit has within it dormant capacities for coping with changes and for growing in loving, communicating, resolving conflict, creating, adventuring, and experiencing happiness. This belief serves a catalytic function of stirring these dormant resources into action. Family members are facilitated not so much in adjusting to but *developing through* life cycle changes. Reuben Hill has called for such a new, developmental model that assists families in "realizing their potentialities . . . *family development* in the sense of a group transcending itself as it moves through the several crises of transition that mark off the major changes in family composition over the life-span."* The very word *enrichment* points to this core tenet, as this word is defined by pioneers of the marriage and family enrichment movement, David and Vera Mace: "We use the term *enrichment,* therefore, not to mean adding something to the ingredients already present in the marriage, like inserting chemicals or vitamins to produce 'enriched' bread, but to describe a facilitating process that will bring into play the existing but inoperative resources that can promote growth and development. Rather than an additive process it is a catalytic process which promotes growth and change that have been inhibited."*

The second principle of this book, that families get blocked at transition points by repetitively applying system-maintaining patterns to new situations, is also taken into consideration by enrichment program leaders. Because of this principle, program leaders involve the entire marriage or family system in the program. In marriage enrichment programs a husband and wife interact together through all the experiences and communicate with each other in depth about varying facets of their relationship. Similarly in family enrichment the members of a family participate together in the activities, having new interactional experiences of each other as a family unit in the present moment of the program. Program leaders are able to utilize the interactional effect of changed family member behavior not only to create new family patterns but also to initiate family momentum toward maintaining behavioral change in new directions.

The third principle, that families draw upon creative resources inside and outside of themselves to find new ways through formerly blocked passageways, is also basic to marriage and family enrichment. In addition to catalyzing dormant capacities for change and growth within couples and families, marriage and family enrichment programs also stimulate change by providing a supportive, growth-encouraging network of other couples and families. Leaders recognize that couples need other couples, and families other families, in order to be strong. Marriage enrichment programs create a climate of group trust and community excitement that encourages couples to experiment with deeper communication and with new approaches to marital interaction. At the close of the event, most leaders encourage participant couples to join or form ongoing support groups, emphasizing that couples need the support of other couples in order to continue the growth patterns begun in the enrichment event.

Similarly family enrichment programs often take the form of "clusters" of families that meet together regularly to care for and support each other.† In family enrichment the individual family is able to observe how other families meet needs and handle conflicts similar to their own, and gain new ideas and values from these other families. Children interact with adults from other families, learning from these alternative adult role models. Above all, the cluster gives the often isolated family a sense of belonging as its members come increasingly to share deeply and meaningfully in this intimate network of families.

The fourth principle of this book, that families are empowered for their change by the Holy Spirit, also plays a significant role in marriage and family enrichment. I believe that it is no accident that the vast majority of marriage and family enrichment programs are sponsored by churches. Not only are churches unique institutions in having access to couples and entire families within their membership, they also have unique resources through which the Spirit is active. Among these resources is the Bible itself, with its words that are "spirit and life." Other resources of the church include a rich heritage of beliefs and symbolic rituals related to major turning points of the family life cycle, such as marriage, birth, and death, and a message concerning forgiveness and reconciliation that has crucial application to marriage and family living.

These resources influence church sponsored marriage and family enrichment programs most directly through the personhood of the program leaders. Because of their Christian faith these leaders have a unique perspective: they view marriage and family living under the direction of the Holy Spirit. As a result these leaders are able to view the human family as uniquely precious, one of God's channels of mediating the experience of grace and trust to humans. At the same time these leaders are able to avoid idolatrizing the family for they realize that the family is not the ultimate goal of human life but only a means to the higher end of human life in relationship to the One who alone is ultimate. Christian leaders influenced by the Spirit's activity also are able to appreciate the wonder of God's intentions for joyful family living while realistically accepting the distortion of all God's intentions by human fallenness and sinfulness. Because of this such leaders do not lay upon participants unattainable, perfectionistic ideals for marriage and family living but stress instead the daily need for accepting the flawed nature of each family member as a sinner in need of the grace and forgiveness of God—and of each other. Finally, such leaders have an air of humility about them stemming from their conviction that the power to transform marriages and families lies beyond human techniques, in the transcendent activity of the Spirit.

The fifth principle of this book, that families are introduced into the change process through metaphoric words, is exercised in marriage and family enrichment programs through the use of experiential education methods. Experiential education involves participants in having experiences and then reflecting upon them. In the language of this book this translates as enabling participants to have experiences that speak to their metaphoric minds and subsequently enabling them to integrate the experiences through rational-mind reflection. Most marriage and family enrichment leaders believe that relational change does not occur simply through receiving new information, so these leaders prefer involving the couples and families in practicing new behaviors instead of relying upon rational techniques such as lecturing. While information about marriage and family relating is valuable, it does not change behavior among family members unless it is acted upon and leads to family members having new experiences of each other.

Techniques of Metaphoric Communication

Such experiences activate the metaphoric minds of participants. The eight techniques of metaphoric communication I explained in chapter 3 can all be employed in experiential exercises in marriage and family enrichment programs, as I will now show in detail.

Active Imagination

As described in chapter 3, the technique of active imagination involves instructing persons to close their eyes, visualize an image, and then act upon that image in some way.

A very powerful active imagination experience during a marriage enrichment program is one in which the married partners imagine experiencing married life from inside their mate's skin. The leaders introduce this experience by describing the general nature of the exercise and inviting everyone to participate to the extent that they feel comfortable. The participants are asked to close their eyes and are guided in a few moments of relaxation. They are then instructed to form inside their mind a detailed image of their partner, as if they were observing their partner across a room. The leaders suggest they notice such details as dress, physical characteristics and mannerisms, and sound of their mate's voice. The direction is next given to imagine entering into the partner's body and physically becoming one's partner, seeing the world through their eyes and experiencing what it feels like to walk around in the partner's body.

While continuing to imagine being their partner, participants are encouraged to experience in detail a series of events that involve marital interaction. The following events are suggested one at a time with a lengthy pause between events: husband and wife meeting at the end of the workday, enjoying a fun time together, being angry in the midst of a conflict, working together, making love, and sharing together a time of worship or deep spiritual experience.

Participants are then asked to imagine leaving their partner's body and once again observing it across the room, noticing their partner's image with new understanding and appreciation. They are then instructed to gradually open their eyes and begin talking quietly with their spouse about what they experienced during this exercise. After a few moments the couples are invited to share with the group of other couples anything they feel comfortable discussing from their active imagination experience or from their discussion with their partner. A good question to ask of husbands is, "What did you discover of your own inner femininity?" and of wives, "What did you discover of your own inner masculinity?"

Another significant active imagination exercise enables family members to have an inner experience of forgiveness. Participants are asked to visualize a picture of another family member who has hurt them in some way, and then imagine all kinds of good things happening to that person. Participants are asked to notice how their own feelings change while watching this picture. This powerful process is explained in detail by the Simontons, who use it in helping cancer patients release resentment and experience forgiving others.*

Yet another active imagination exercise is to ask each participating family to select an image that came out of a dream of one of their family members (or from some other source, such as a favorite family story). Participants are then asked to close their eyes and to interact with that image. When all have finished, members are asked to share their experiences within the family group. Groups of families may then compare and discuss their experiences.

Stories, Parables, and Dreams

The telling of stories, parables, and dreams enables enrichment group leaders to communicate on several levels of meaning to the metaphoric minds of their listeners, who are free to translate the message into relevance for their own lives. Particularly effective with persons of all ages are popular children's stories. For example, I have often told in either marriage or family retreats Dr. Seuss's *Horton Hears a Who* with its affirmation of the worth of every human person "no matter how small."

Any form of story is useful in enrichment settings, whether fairy tale, biblical parable, folk fable, or a short story by a famous writer, for example, D. H. Lawrence's "The Rocking Horse Winner." The telling of a story can be followed by having couples or family members discuss together its relevance for their lives, fantasize further from it—such as writing a new ending—or enact it in symbolic, ritualistic fashion. For example, in the closing worship of marriage enrichment retreats I have often told the tale about the rabbi who is shown the difference between heaven and hell, the residents of heaven having "learned one simple skill . . . how to feed one another."* The retreat participants are then invited to enact this metaphoric message by communing their spouse in the sacramental act of the Lord's Supper or by mutually feeding each other in a concluding love feast.

Dreams provide rich material for enrichment events. Family members can be encouraged to relate their dreams to each other and to discuss their meaning. One family enrichment leader I know has all the families in a family workshop pool their dreams and then choose one of them that seems to have significance for all the families. The leader then asks the whole community of families to participate in a dramatic reenactment of the entire dream.

It is important that leaders of marriage and family enrichment programs also share from their own life stories and their own dreams. Participants are eager to hear how these leader couples have struggled with common problems in their own marriage and family living and what they have done to seek to resolve them. Persons struggling in a family life cycle passageway can identify with a leader's own story of being blocked in that passage and finding a new way through. Leaders who listen sensitively to their own dreams encourage participants to follow their example by respecting and attending to the productions of their own metaphoric minds.

Reframing

Reframing, as I have defined it in the preceding chapter, involves changing the frame of meaning within which a problem has been defined so that the problem is seen in a new light.

One of the areas of married life in which my wife and I utilize reframing when we are coleading a marriage enrichment experience is that of "giving love." Many couples block themselves in this area of marriage by framing it within either a metaphor of love as "trying hard" to give to one's partner or the contrasting metaphor of blaming one's partner for *not* giving. Within both of these frames the result is the same: the partners become "given out," tired and resentful. They feel anything but loving. In a lecturette we as leaders reframe loving as grounded in a focus not upon giving but upon *receiving* love, that is, fully sensing, enjoying, and appreciating the person, touch, and gifts of one's partner. The more partners are thus receiving or "taking in," the more they find themselves spontaneously giving back to their partners, and the very enjoyment of their partner's touch or gift is itself a giving of love. The result can be an experience of a balance of giving and receiving love, like the metaphor of the righteous in Psalm 1 as being like a tree planted by streams of water, able to give forth fruit abundantly because it is continually receiving. We then invite the couples to experience this reframing by taking turns with their spouse in the roles of giver and receiver in such activities as a back rub, face caress, or the exchange of self-created gifts.

Power in relationships is another area in which we utilize reframing in both marriage and family enrichment. Some parents or spouses tend to frame power or the attempts to influence others as unloving behavior. Other parents or spouses adopt an opposite metaphor that one must always have control of the power in relationships to avoid being weak or taken advantage of. The frequent result of either of these approaches is that family members find themselves caught in covert or overt power struggles among themselves.

Again in a lecturette, we as leaders reframe using power as essential to loving others. Only as we respect and value ourselves by expressing our real needs do the other family members experience being respected and valued by us. We add that such exercise of power needs to be balanced by a willingness to share power with and yield power to the other members. To those who protest the importance of being strong and in control of one's feelings or relationships, we add a reframing question, "Can you be strong enough to be weak?"

In a family enrichment setting we often facilitate participants to further integrate this reframing through an experience of giving one or more of the children in the family the power to decide upon and lead the family in an activity, such as a walk, game, or discussion. An alternative is to have family members take turns in the role of mother in a game of "Mother May I?" Family members are then invited to share their feelings of being in roles of power or powerlessness.

Special Language Patterns

The effectiveness of reframing can be heightened by phrasing the message to be communicated in some of the special language patterns described in chapter 3, such as aphorisms, quotations, and marking.

For example, when I am addressing a marriage enrichment group about the importance of receiving love I often quote David Ireland's statement (slightly modified): "Persons are made happy not by the amount of love they are given but by the amount they allow themselves to *receive.*"*

Similarly when discussing power in marriage or family relationships the aphorism attributed to Robert Johann can be quoted: "Love without power is not enough because love without power soon ceases to be love." To seed the point about yielding power a leader can cite St. Paul's terse maxim, "My strength is made perfect in weakness."

Jokes, puns, and humorous anecdotes from the leader's own family life are particularly effective in communicating truths about family relating. My wife and I never tire of recounting to other couples our early struggle for power on our first trip to the grocery store as married partners where we fiercely debated the earth-shaking decision of whether to purchase whole milk or powdered milk!

Creative Memory

In creative memory participants are asked to recall past experiences in which they exercised qualities that can be utilized in their current relationships. The effect of this creative recall is that married partners or family members come to view each other in the present moment as possessing those same resources.

An example of the use of this technique in marriage enrichment is a "peak experiences" exercise. Participants are asked to close their eyes, relax, and begin to recall the happiest, most positive and deeply meaningful experiences they have shared with their spouse in the course of their entire relationship. Participants are encouraged to linger in each memory, recalling such details as what they saw, heard, and felt during the experience. When they have finished, participants are encouraged to open their eyes and jot down on paper a list of the events and any details that were particularly outstanding. The leaders then encourage each couple to go apart from the others for twenty or thirty minutes to compare their lists and their memories of these experiences.

Similarly in family enrichment the members of a family can participate in a "family strengths" exercise. Each member is asked to recall all the strengths, special talents, and unique qualities possessed by themselves and each family member, as exemplified in particular moments in the life of the family. Next each member is to recall the same resources possessed by the family as a unit, together with special moments in which the family displayed these strengths. Family members then make a list together of the strengths they have remembered individually. The family can be given the further task of planning how to use and develop one or more of these strengths in the days ahead. If possible the family is encouraged to carry out one facet of that plan during the enrichment workshop.

This exercise can also be used for couples toward the close of a marriage enrichment event as a "marriage strengths" exercise.

In both marriage and family enrichment retreats, we place in the center of the group an "imagination center," a table full of objects associated with childhood play, such as toys, dolls, and crayons. At the opening of the retreat, participants are asked to focus on the table and recall memories of favorite childhood toys or play experiences, then share them with the group. This enables participants to access their inner resources for learning through playful creativity and imagination. The imagination center again becomes the focus of attention as an altar in the closing worship service. Participants are asked to relate objects on the table to significant new learnings they have experienced during the retreat.

Action Imperatives

Action imperatives are instructions given to participants to do some activity. Carrying out the instructions leads the participants to draw upon latent resources within themselves.

Resources of increased caring between married partners and family members can be called upon by a "caring exchange" exercise. The leader gives all participants paper and pencil and instructs them to write down a brief list of small but specific caring actions that other family members could do for them. The criteria for items on the list include that the caring actions be those that the writer would feel very pleased to receive, that they are doable during the enrichment event or in the following ten days, and that they are relatively inexpensive. Each participant compiles a separate list for each family member involved and then hands them the list. The leader instructs participants to select only one item off of each list they have received and to perform that action within the event or the following week. This small act can generate an increased caring in the family as it unleashes the resources within all members to care for each other.

Another use of imperative to action in marriage and family

enrichment is relational sculpting. The leaders instruct the married partners or family members to take turns nonverbally arranging the other members of their family in a living tableau which portrays how they relate to one another. Each family member sculpts the interrelationships of the family from his or her perspective, showing such dimensions as closeness and distance, alliances, and patterns of interaction. All the family members can then discuss the feelings they experience while in their place inside the sculpture. Finally, all members of the family are given opportunity to form a new sculpture that symbolizes how they would want the family to be if they could change it to be anything they desire.

Various ritual imperatives are also possible in enrichment events. I have earlier mentioned family members communing one another in an informal closing worship. Such a worship event can also include a forgiveness ritual. The couple or family can be instructed to go apart from the group and in private take turns with each member saying to each other member, "I have hurt you by . . .", adding one action or attitude by which they believe they have caused that member unhappiness. The listening member is asked to respond in such words as "I forgive you as God forgives you," and may then seal the forgiveness with a hand clasp or hug.

Probably the most common action imperative used in enrichment programs is the dialogue, in which spouses or family members are instructed in principles of how to communicate with each other and then asked to engage in conversation with each other on a selected topic, utilizing the suggested principles. Much has been written about the use of this technique.* While some leaders have couples or family members dialogue privately apart from the rest of the group, other leaders have them dialogue in the presence of one or more other couples or families who can subsequently give feedback and encouragement.

Affirmations

Affirmations, or positive, personal expressions, form one of the most powerful means of enriching relationships.

In a marriage enrichment event partners can experience an

affirmation sharing. The leaders instruct the participants to think carefully about their partner for several minutes, focusing upon the personal qualities that they most love and cherish about them as the unique human being they are and upon the actions they do that they most appreciate and value. The participants are asked to write down in key word notes those qualities and actions that come to mind, keeping these notes out of their partner's sight. When everyone is finished, the leaders demonstrate how they would like the participants to share this information with their partner: the partners face each other, maintaining eye and hand contact, and take turns being "giver" and "receiver," the giver sharing his or her entire list. Special instructions are given for the receiver role, including listening without interrupting and taking every affirmation fully to heart without questioning or analyzing it. When both partners are finished they are given time to share their feelings.

This same affirmation exercise is also very effective in a family enrichment setting. Each family member prepares a list of affirmations for every other family member, and each dyad within the family (such as father-daughter, husband-wife) takes a turn sitting in the middle of the family circle exchanging their affir-mations. Small children may need a parent or older sibling to coach them in preparing their lists.

Play

Playful activities engaged in for the sake of sheer fun are at the heart of marriage and family enrichment. Adults and children alike engaged in carefree play find their metaphoric minds awakened and learning rapidly.

My wife and I often open a marriage enrichment program with the statement, "Marriage enrichment is adult play." We soon illustrate what we mean by involving everybody in one or more children's games. All adults have at one time been children and can engage in such games as "Fruit Basket Upset" or "Drop the Handkerchief." The playing of simple games interspersed throughout a marriage enrichment program stimulates a spon-taneous, playful atmosphere.

We always have a collection of children's toys around for

spontaneous play or discussion starters. One not-so-spontaneous use of toys is an exercise involving tinker toys. Each couple is instructed to create out of tinker toys a symbolic expression of their marriage. When all have finished, the couples are invited to share with other couples the meaning they have expressed— intentionally or nonintentionally—through the symbol they have created.

A further use of this last exercise is to have partners discuss with each other the process they went through in deciding what to build and in actually creating the symbol. The leaders suggest that the couple ask themselves what this process says about the way they ordinarily make decisions, influence each other, and work together throughout their relationship.

One of the most important dimensions of family enrichment is the experience of adults and children playing together, especially children seeing their own parents at play. Every kind of children's game from "Four Corners" to "Gossip" can be delightful for this purpose, as well as active games like volleyball and all kinds of relays. Also very useful are playful means of expression involving family members together in such activities as finger painting, clay sculpting, enacting skits, and drawing.

A good early exercise for a family enrichment group is to assign each family to create a family drawing using crayons and newsprint. It can either be a free drawing of their own choice or an assigned creation such as dividing a paper into four squares with each square portraying a theme, such as: something unique about our family, a way we have fun as a family, a funny thing that happened to us, and something that is important to our family. When the drawings are finished the families can show and explain their creations to other families.

Programming for Enrichment

How can these varied techniques be fitted together into a marriage or family enrichment program? The combination of activities that forms any particular program will grow out of the unique needs of the participants and purposes of their leaders, but I will give a sample format for a marriage enrichment weekend and for a family enrichment evening that my wife and I might lead. I will first sketch only the bare framework of exercises, utilizing those that I have described above. Afterward I will discuss some other factors that need to be considered in planning these kinds of events.

Format for a Marriage Enrichment Weekend

Friday evening
Creative Memory: "Imagination center"
Story: Children's story leading into purposes of the weekend
Play: Children's game
Creative Memory: "Peak experiences"
Action Imperative: Couple dialogue

Saturday morning
Active Imagination: Using an image from a dream or story
Action Imperative: "Caring exchange"
Play: Tinker toys—symbol of marriage
Reframing/Special Language Patterns: Lecturette on power
Action Imperative: Couple dialogue on a conflict issue

Saturday afternoon
Play: Couple free time plus group active play such as volleyball
Creative Memory: Couples recall positive sexual experiences
Story: Leaders share their own struggles and growth in their sexual relationship
Action Imperative: Couple dialogue about their sexual relationship

Saturday evening
Active Imagination: Inside partner's skin
Reframing/Special Language Patterns: Lecturette on receiving love
Affirmation: Affirmation sharing
Play: Games and free time

Sunday morning
Creative Memory: "Marriage strengths"

Action Imperative: Couple dialogue

All techniques: Closing informal worship

("imagination center," stories related to marriage growth, sharing affirmations from the weekend, exchanging gifts, forgiveness and communion rituals, etc.)

Format for a Family Enrichment Evening

(This would be the first of a series of eight meetings on the theme "Working Together as a Family." The following seven meetings would follow a similar format.)

Creative Memory: "Imagination center"

Play: Active game such as "Fruit Basket Upset"

Story/Parable/Dream: Story such as *Horton Hears a Who* that introduces the theme and leads into leaders defining purposes

Play: Family drawing in four squares

Action Imperative: Family dialogue on the theme and reflecting upon the drawing exercise

Several techniques: Closing informal worship

Among the numerous factors to be considered in planning for an enrichment event, attention needs to be paid especially to program structure, format, leadership, participant recruitment, and setting.

The structure of the program requires thoughtful planning. Most enrichment leaders advocate some combination of intensive weekend programs with ongoing periodic meetings. Programs that take place over an entire weekend tend to stimulate a more intense emotional involvement, heighten motivation to grow, and encourage a greater depth of relationship, while ongoing programs that meet weekly or bimonthly over an extended time period allow for the integration of new learnings in everyday marriage and family living. In our experience weekend formats seem to work out less well for family groups, as children tire out from concentrated activity. Any weekend program for couples or families needs to provide for followup activity for participants in order for the growth initiated on the weekend to be sustained.

The format of enrichment programs should be planned to allow for flexibility and for variation in types of activity. Leaders need to be ready to shift the program direction or change planned events in response to feedback from the participants or observation of group activity. The design of the program should provide variation between active, stimulating events and more quiet, reflective times, between metaphoric and rational processes, and between intracouple or family involvement and sharing in the total community of couples or families. Opening events of the enrichment program should be chosen for creating among the participants and leaders a climate of trust and of relaxed fun. Closing events need to be designed to prepare participants for reentering the world of their daily living and for planning to continue their growth by carrying out specific activities.

A primary consideration in planning for an enrichment event is choosing the leaders. A male-female coleadership team is needed in order to provide identification for participants of both sexes and to model dyadic interaction. It is even better if the leaders are a married couple for they can also share their ongoing growth struggles in their own marriage and family. The leaders need to be trained for the specialized function of facilitating marriage or family enrichment groups. Such training is now becoming widely available through national enrichment programs and national church bodies.*

Qualities particularly desirable in leaders include ongoing investment in their own marital and family growth, trust and utilization of the intuitive, imaginative properties of their own metaphoric minds, and reliance upon the Holy Spirit in their own lives and in facilitating the growth of others.

Recruitment of participants is a factor that requires much time and effort. I have learned that the most effective means of recruitment is to gather a core of two or three enthused couples who plan to participate in the program themselves and ask them to recruit other couples or families by face-to-face contact. The information they share and all more formal publicity should emphasize that the program is a positive educational experience, not a problem-focused or therapy event. If the intention is to have a fairly intimate fellowship it is preferable to recruit a group of no more than six to ten couples for marriage enrichment or four to six families for family enrichment. In the family program it is helpful to have persons from varying age levels and types of family structure, such as one-parent families and couples without children as well as two-parent families. However, consideration needs to be given to having children of comparable ages within the group so that each child can feel, "There is someone my age I can relate to here."

The setting of the program should be carefully selected to insure comfort and privacy. For a weekend program the preferred setting is a residential retreat center in which participants can be completely away from their normal routine and setting. Private bedrooms for couples are essential. For a program meeting weekly a large, carpeted room in the local church is satisfactory.

While it is apparent that preparing for and conducting such an enrichment program requires considerable investment of time and energy, the benefits couples and families realize in the release of their growth potential are worth the investment. At least this is the testimony of many enrichment group participants, who join with my son in his evaluation, "Daddy, I feel happy!"

5. Family Life Cycle Education

Oscar, an oyster, was enjoying a very fine life. Then one day he noticed an irritating pain. It came from a grain of sand having become caught between his shell and his stomach. It hurt very much. Oscar wondered what to do. At first he thought that if he ignored the pain it might go away. So he closed his eyes and concentrated with all his might on ignoring the pain. When he finally opened his eyes he noticed that the pain was still there.

Oscar became furious. He threw a temper tantrum and swore with all the cursewords in his oyster vocabulary. And when he was all done he noticed that the pain was still there.

At this point Oscar broke down and began to cry. He felt totally helpless. Oscar cried and cried, and when he was all through crying he noticed that the pain was still there.

Just then along came Esther, another oyster. Oscar told her his difficulty. Esther paused for a moment and then responded, "I cannot help you. But there is something you know—but have forgotten that you know—that can help. And when you remember it you will be able to take care of this problem."

Suddenly Oscar remembered that God had given him a very special ability. He had the power deep within him to secrete a mysterious fluid. Oscar decided to use this power, and he secreted a fluid that flowed all around the grain of sand. Later the fluid dried and hardened. And then Oscar noticed that there had formed around the grain of sand a beautiful pearl, one of the most precious of all jewels! Oscar was proud, very satisfied with himself—and deeply grateful.

I frequently tell this little story in family life cycle education programs. Oscar's story points to the central thrust of this educational form: to enable family members to remember what they know, that is, to rediscover God-given resources to cope with the changes that occur at turning points of the life cycle. Family life cycle education is a class or workshop in which adults learn concepts and attitudes about life transitions and develop resources and skills for growing through them. While these concepts and resources are primarily addressed to the normal, expectable transitions in the family life cycle, they are also applied to more unexpected transitions such as loss of a job or loss of a loved one through divorce or accidental death. This educational form differs from the family enrichment programs described in the preceding chapter by being designed primarily for adults and by placing a greater emphasis upon conveying informational content and teaching specific skills.

Objectives

The objectives of a family life cycle education class or workshop closely parallel the five major themes of this book.

The first and most basic objective of the program is to influence participants to develop constructive attitudes toward life cycle changes. Two such attitudes are: (*a*) change is a normal, expected part of family life, for families are moving, developing entities; and (*b*) it is possible to cope effectively with change and increase one's life satisfaction. Participants can learn, along with Oscar, that grains of sand come into all our lives and that there are things we can do to transform these grains into new realities, leaving us very satisfied.

A second objective of the program is to convey to participants information about life cycle transitions. Giving family members information about what to expect in an approaching life cycle passageway can help them anticipate experiences they will encounter and new developmental tasks they will need to master. Perhaps if Oscar had received anticipatory information about grains of sand and their effect on him he would have felt less overwhelmed by his developmental crisis.

A third objective of family life cycle education is to help participants use internal and external resources to cope with and grow through the blocked passageway. Family members are enabled through the program to rediscover dormant internal resources for coping. They are also directed to develop external support systems and to practice behavioral-action skills useful for moving through the passage. Not only did Oscar remember his dormant capacity for dealing with grains of sand, he also acted upon it. When he did so he found himself beyond the passage.

A fourth objective is to enable participants to integrate their transition experience in a spiritual understanding of the meaning of their lives. Reliance upon the Holy Spirit's activity in empowering transformation is encouraged. Family members, not unlike Oscar, need finally to let go of their futile attempts to change a grain of sand and rely upon God-given resources that facilitate a transformation. As Oscar concluded with a deep sense of gratitude, so family members at the end of a transition can come to understand more deeply the meaning of God's intervention in their lives.

A final program objective is to use metaphoric communication to catalyze the resources of the metaphoric minds of participants for coping with their life changes. Esther's healing words about remembering "something that you know" triggered Oscar's metaphoric-mind resources. The variety of techniques described in the two previous chapters are useful throughout this educational program, as I will show in the next section.

Program Themes

The five objectives of family life cycle education can be accomplished through a program that focuses in succession upon five themes: attitudes, information, resources, action, and integration.* These five themes can form the content for a five-session evening class or be distributed throughout a weekend workshop. I will now introduce each of the themes and suggest some metaphoric communication techniques for developing them.

Attitudes

The opening event of the program is designed to introduce the first major objective: to influence participants to develop constructive attitudes toward life cycle changes. A research team that studied people's coping with life transitions discovered that personal attitudes toward life change vary all the way from a sense of active inner control over one's life direction to complete helplessness.* The researchers concluded that the attitudes a person holds are the chief determinant in shaping how that person reacts to a transition. If family members feel surprised by the effects of a change and powerless to do anything to cope with them, they are unlikely to take constructive action. If, however, they accept change as a normal, expected part of life and believe that they have coped with such changes before—and can do so again—they are more likely to act in ways that cause them to grow through the transition.

Techniques in metaphoric communication can be used to begin building such constructive attitudes, for example, the technique that was referred to in chapter 3 as story/parable/dream. The leaders can open the session by telling one or a series of carefully chosen stories that seed the idea—change is an inevitable, ongoing part of family life. "The Tale of the Sands" cited in chapter 1 is one possibility. An alternative is to retell the life stories of biblical personages, such as Abraham and his family, Job, or Paul. The leaders may also want to share some of their own dreams.

Other useful techniques might include creative memory and play. The leaders ask class members to close their eyes and begin to review their life journey in memory. Suggestions are given to visualize their very earliest memory, all the significant turning points of their lives, high peaks as well as deep valleys along the way, and significant persons who have influenced the course of their lives. Participants then open their eyes and are given a long piece of newsprint and crayons or pastels. They are invited to draw their life journey from its beginning to the present, giving special attention to the key turning points.

When all have finished, the leaders hand out a series of questions for each participant to reflect upon as they apply to several of the turning points in their journey. The questions may include: What were some of the ingredients of this new desert or life passageway? What attitudes, personal abilities, other-person resources, and actions did I use to cope with the changes? What may the Holy Spirit have been teaching me through this life transition?

In addition to utilizing these techniques in the opening session, leaders also use lecturettes and small group discussion to help participants integrate key ideas related to the importance of attitudes in responding to life change.

Information

Two bodies of information can be conveyed in this second section of the program: an overview of the family life cycle as a whole and a description of the sequential pattern of responses persons experience in going through a particular life transition.

The first body of information can include a description of the stages of the family life cycle such as is found in chapter 2, with particular attention given to the tasks of each stage. Most detail needs to be conveyed for those life stages class participants are in or about to enter.

The second body of information, response patterns in a particular transition, may be conveyed by describing the model developed by Adams, Hayes, and Hopson in their book *Transitions*.* These authors suggest that persons going through a transition will experience a cycle of personal reactions and feelings composed of seven phases: (*a*) immobilization, feeling frozen and unable to think clearly or to act; (*b*) minimization, denying or minimizing the changes in order to allow a person to regroup internally and find strength to comprehend the impact of the transition; (*c*) depression, facing the reality of what has occurred and feeling the weight of the real losses involved; (*d*) acceptance, letting go of the past situation as gone and experiencing a willingness to accept the new situation as being reality; (*e*) testing, trying out new actions and feeling a surge of energy to cope with the new situation; (*f*) search for meaning, reflecting upon the changed situation in order to understand its significance for one's life; and (*g*) internalization, integrating these meanings and new actions into one's lifestyle. The authors point out, of course, that persons do not move neatly in order from one phase to another but rather have their own unique pattern of moving back and forth through these responses.

Conveying this rational-mind information needs to be complemented with metaphoric communication. Once again storytelling can play a helpful role.

The most useful approach is for the leaders to tell their own life stories. I once had the opportunity to ask Carl Whitaker, the family therapist, how families get past where they are blocked. He replied, "I don't know how people change, but I know how I have changed." On another occasion I asked Milton Erickson a similar question about how he would help people move through a life transition. His answer was, "I tell them about my transitions, because that's how people learn." He remembered telling his own life story to a man going through a crisis, and the man later told him, "The story of your changes gave me an understanding of the changes I would have to make."

The story of Oscar, the oyster, provides another useful technique for communicating the response cycle. Families find it interesting to trace Oscar's movement through each of the seven phases.

Besides storytelling, the techniques referred to in chapter 3 as special language patterns and reframing can also be effective. Putting emphasis upon the quotation of Esther's words to Oscar makes use of the special language patterns of nonreferring phrases and marking: "There is *something* you know . . . and when you *remember* it you will be able to take care of this problem."

In discussing the cycle of responses to a transition, it is useful to show that the various experiences of loss involved in a transition have potential gains inherent in them as well. Depression can be described as a helpful friend, and the expression I quoted in chapter 3 can be cited: "when going to pieces holds you together."

Resources

The third section of the program focuses upon enabling participants to rediscover their own resources for coping with changes. These resources are of two kinds.

Internal Resources

Attention is first given to internal resources. One of the most useful means for coping with the external pressures that accompany change is for a person to focus inwardly. This enables the person to screen out stress-producing external factors and simultaneously tap into the creative, healing resources of the metaphoric mind. Some of the metaphoric-mind techniques can be taught to class participants for them to use themselves as practiced tools for coping during transition periods.

One thinks in this connection particularly of the technique I have called active imagination. Leaders can teach participants one or more means of thorough relaxation and then encourage them to form inwardly a visual image that symbolizes for them the major stress or difficulty they are experiencing in the transition, such as Mary's "burden" in chapter 3. The leaders then encourage participants to allow their imagination to act on the image until a full resolution of the imaged difficulty occurs. If some class members experience the stress bodily, they can be encouraged to image in detail the affected part of the body and then image another bodily part acting on that until the hurting part is relieved or healed. For example, Watzlawick describes an obese person vividly imaging a picture of his body fat as round, yellowish white cells stacked in layers and being attacked by proteins in the shape of little animals until they are devoured and their energy released.* A physician, Robert Anderson, describes an exercise he gives his patients in which they visualize the control center of the autonomic nervous system sending out messages to reduce tension and regulate energy levels in all parts of the body.†

Creative memory is another potentially helpful technique. Building upon the life journey exercise described above in the section on Attitudes, leaders can ask group members to close their eyes and remember in detail three past occasions in which they coped creatively with a change and experienced feelings of satisfaction. The leaders then suggest that the part of each person that was active in those experiences can be given the verbal label "the Creative Coper," a part that can be called upon in dealing with any future change. Participants may then be asked to imagine employing their Creative Coper in a transition they are currently anticipating. Throughout the rest of the class, leaders can occasionally refer to the Creative Coper inside each participant.

Another technique well worth considering in this connection is affirmation. Participants are asked to "listen in" to their own internal dialogue, the stream of "self-talk" messages they are continually expressing to themselves. The leaders instruct members to write down any repetitious negative messages they detect, especially those related to making a transition. The leaders then assist participants to write a positive restatement of each negative message in the form of an affirmation. For example, the negative self-message "I just don't have what it takes" might become "As I am learning to rely upon my own inner resources my self-confidence is growing stronger and stronger." "I've got no future to look forward to anymore" may become "I am learning to picture a future full of promise and hope." Class members are encouraged to memorize and repeat frequently every day their affirmations while visualizing themselves accomplishing the positive goal in a detailed image.

External Resources

After dealing with developing internal resources, leaders turn to external coping resources. They emphasize the importance of regular physical exercise, exerting the body at least three times a week to the point that one's resting pulse rate is doubled for at least five minutes. Equally important is cultivating supportive relationships with a variety of people. Persons having difficulty moving through a passageway often report feeling isolated or unsupported.

In this connection the technique known as action imperative takes on a special importance. The leaders ask class members to write on the left side of a piece of paper the names of all persons with whom they have regular face-to-face contact. Members are then asked to rate the quality of positive emotional support they receive from each of these persons by putting a number to the right of each name, ranging from 0 as "negative" to 4 as "very positive." Next, to the right of these numbers members are to estimate the average number of hours per month spent with each person. Finally, members are asked to review the page and reflect upon the quality of emotional support they are currently experiencing and to decide if there are any specific changes they would like to make in their support system. Participants meet with a partner to brainstorm and create an action plan for changing or strengthening their external resources. Leaders may make input by suggesting organized support groups in the community, such as self-help groups.

Action

The fourth section of the program grows out of the objective to develop behavioral-action skills in utilizing external resources to move through a life passageway. The changed circumstances brought about by a transition require persons to make and implement important decisions. Being able to make wise choices and to act upon them increases persons' sense of having control over the direction of their lives.

Story is again a useful technique. In opening this fourth section a leader can relate the narrative of "The Overcoat," a short story by Nikolai Gogol.* It has a powerful message about an individual who by making a decision and acting upon it was transformed into a new and more vital person.

The technique of action imperative may also be used. Leaders can teach participants a rational decision-making and implementation process by having them select one decision area in a current transition and apply a series of skills to it. Skills focused upon in this exercise may include: defining the need, goal formulation, brainstorming alternatives, selecting an action, planning for implementation, and implementation.†

Exercises involving active imagination may prove useful. When participants have the outcome goal of a decision in mind the leaders ask them to visualize in detail being in the future and living out that chosen goal. They are encouraged to enjoy all the pleasant feelings and satisfactions of having achieved that outcome. Next, the leaders direct them to visualize in their imagination going through all the steps they took getting to that outcome, moving backward from the outcome experience to the present moment. Participants may then be invited to share this experience with a partner in the class.

A variation of this exercise can be used for persons trying to decide between two choices. Participants are asked to visualize in detail in the future having made one of the choices, paying attention to all of their feelings in that experience. When finished participants repeat this procedure with the second choice. Participants then describe both experiences to a partner in the class, comparing and contrasting the two. The participants may then feed information from this exercise back into the preceding rational decision-making procedure.

Integration

The final section of the program is aimed toward enabling participants to integrate their transition experiences and new learnings in a framework of meaning. Particular emphasis is given to helping them integrate their life experiences with their own interpretation of life's meaning from a spiritual perspective. In the cycle of responses to transitions noted earlier, humans have a need to make meaning out of their experiences and to internalize that meaning in their lifestyle.

Creative memory and play can be helpful in this connection. Prior to the last meeting of the class, participants are given the homework task of writing an autobiography from the future perspective of the last year of their life. They are asked to note the interaction of their Creative Coper with the succession of life transition challenges of the family life cycle and to reflect upon the activity of the Holy Spirit at these turning points. They are further encouraged to discover and develop a core life theme that gives meaning to their life story. As an alternative to writing, group members can choose some other mode of creative expression for this task, such as painting, sculpture, or poetry. In the closing meeting participants are invited to share their creations with one another in small groups.

The techniques of reframing and special language patterns also enter the picture. In a summary lecturette and in responding to members' questions leaders help make meaning by casting old issues in a new light. For example, to the question often in class members' minds—"How does the emphasis on actively coping with life changes fit with the need to let go and rely upon the Holy Spirit?"—I often respond by quoting Paul's admonition that captures both sides of this paradox, "Work out your own salvation with fear and trembling; for God is at work in you" (Phil. 2:12–13).

A whole variety of techniques can figure into the closing informal worship. The purpose of this last activity is to give participants opportunity to express gratitude to God for his transforming activity in their lives. I sometimes quote a man I once met who said that he came to faith after a most fortunate event occurred in his life and the realization hit him, "I have no one to whom to say thank you." Leaders may share stories from the world's literature of persons who made life changes and found new meaning, such as Dickens' Scrooge and Wilde's Selfish Giant. Opportunity may also be given for group members to share affirmations of each other and to participate in an informal communion or love feast.

In planning a family life cycle education program all the factors involved in planning enrichment programs I listed in the preceding chapter need to be considered.* An ongoing class of five or more weekly meetings may be more helpful than a weekend workshop, for the additional time between sessions gives participants more opportunity to reflect upon and apply new learnings to their lives. The size of the class can be expanded if there are additional leaders available so that the total group can be regularly broken down into smaller units for discussion. A variation of the program structure is to design the class for persons all experiencing the same developmental crisis, such as middle age or marital separation. All the content is then tailored to dealing in depth with this one turning point.

6. Pastoral Family Therapy

Pastor Taylor felt overwhelmed. He had known that the Baker family was going to drop in to see him sometime this afternoon at the church, but they had come earlier than he expected. He had hastily dismissed his secretary and found chairs for Mr. and Mrs. Baker, their school-age boys Todd and Randy, and pre-school daughter Teresa. Pastor Taylor had no more than sat down when Mrs. Baker launched into a description of a series of problems she and her husband were having with the children's disruptive behavior at home, school, church, and in the neighborhood. As Pastor Taylor tried to grasp one problem, he was confused by Mrs. Baker's giving details of still another problem that seemed unconnected to the first. His confusion wasn't helped by Mr. Baker occasionally interrupting his wife to add unrelated details. The pastor's concentration was further impaired by Todd and Randy angrily poking and kicking at each other, and Teresa running about the room singing to herself. At one point Mrs. Baker turned and verbally attacked her husband. The two were soon in an argument that grew increasingly heated. Pastor Taylor experienced a helpless, sinking feeling in his stomach. Suddenly he heard a crash behind him. Everyone turned to discover that Teresa had just knocked over a flowerpot stand. The shattered pot and its contents were now strewn all over the floor.

What one of us has not had an experience like that of Pastor Taylor! We can readily identify with his feelings of being overwhelmed, helpless. Sitting in a room with a troubled family often feels like being the driver of a runaway stagecoach, and we have lost the reins.

What a clergy or lay helping person needs in order to get back the reins and bring order out of chaos in a family meeting is an organized, systematic approach to family change. That is how I would define pastoral family therapy: it is an organized, purposeful therapeutic intervention aimed to assist a family to change—under the power of the Holy Spirit. It is those last seven words that make this approach pastoral.

A Pastoral Approach

A therapist who has a pastoral orientation is one who views all therapy or healing action as effected by the activity of the Holy Spirit and as resulting in rendering the lives of family members more meaningful in relation to God's purpose for human life. The pastoral therapist communicates metaphoric, healing words that place the responsibility for their enactment upon the metaphoric minds of family members. The therapist then relaxes for his or her job is done. The pastoral therapist knows that the Holy Spirit alone can now act upon the seed that has been sown to effect the miracle of growth.

The family therapy approach I am presenting here combines right- and left-brain activity. The right-brain aspect centers in therapists relying upon their own metaphoric-mind resources. The left-brain dimension is expressed through a systematic conceptual framework and a systematic intervention methodology. Both dimensions are essential.

The Role of Trust

First, then, the right-brain dimension. I believe that the essential key to effective family therapy lies in therapists trusting their own metaphoric minds.

Therapists do this by receiving the metaphoric communication of family members within the therapists' own right brains, tuning in to their own inner fantasies and feelings evoked by their experience of the clients. The therapists then trust their own intuitive, creative right-brain resources to respond in metaphoric communication toward the family. This communication is addressed directly to the metaphoric minds of the family members in an almost telepathic fashion.

Because the therapists are trusting their own selves, they are also able to share transparently their own life experiences. Metaphoric communication of the therapists' life stories awakens in the minds of family members echoes of what they already intuitively know from their own earlier experiences. These intuitive echoes provide directions for family transformation.

Further, through loving trust of themselves therapists are enabled to share transparently their own caring for family members. The expression of this caring catalyzes family members' rediscovering their capacities for feeling and expressing nurturing love for each other. Carl Whitaker writes of the family therapist: "He looks across the room and sees a person whom he sees as like part of himself, and he feels loving toward that person and expresses that feeling. Such moments of encounter can be quietly and wonderfully powerful, and they are all the more exciting for the fact that the whole family is watching and learning." Whitaker adds that this event triggers further expressions of loving in the session and that these are "the core events in family therapy."*

Pastoral family therapists are able to have this kind of trustful, loving connection with themselves because they in turn stand in trustful relationship with God. Family members experience trust for and from such therapists because these therapists are relying upon a transcendent Lover who alone is fully trustworthy.

In summary, the right-brain dimension of family therapy centers in therapists so fully trusting their God and their own inmost metaphoric resources that they provide family members with powerful experiences that release their abilities to trust themselves. Therapists growing in their own trust and inner vitality are contagious, infecting clients with their energy. One way I seek to grow in this dimension myself is to begin each day of counseling with a period of meditation in which I repeat the affirmation "I am learning to rely upon God through my metaphoric mind to provide everything I need to do my counseling."

Thinking and Doing

The left-brain aspect of this approach to family therapy includes two elements: (1) a conceptual framework that enables therapists to organize their understanding of any particular family and how it can change, and (2) an intervention methodology that tells therapists how to proceed in carrying out family therapy. In short, the approach tells how to think and to do family therapy. The therapy will then have purposeful direction, which increases therapist self-confidence and the family's confidence in the therapist. This confidence enables therapists and families together to move intentionally toward mutually set goals as partners who respect and learn from each other.

A Conceptual Framework

Let us look first at the thinking dimension of a pastoral family therapy approach. A useful conceptual framework needs to answer four questions: (1) What is a family, and how does it function effectively? (2) How does a family malfunction? (3) How does a family change in order to restore effective functioning? (4) How can family change be facilitated by therapeutic intervention?

Every helping person needs to work out his or her own unique answers to these questions, forming a conceptual statement that is congruent with the helper's own personality, life experience, and personal convictions. The answers that currently fit for me and serve as my guiding conceptual framework are summarized in the first chapter of this book. Briefly, I answer the questions this way: (1) A family is a moving, changing system that uses basic metaphors to direct its development through the life cycle. (2) A family begins to malfunction when it repetitively applies old approaches from its established metaphors to a changed situation in a new life cycle passageway. (3) A family changes by discovering a new, metaphor-transforming way through the passageway, enlightened and activated by the Holy Spirit. (4) A therapist facilitates this change by intervening with metaphorical communication aimed at changing the family's metaphors. This framework helps me to organize my thinking about any particular family that comes to talk to me and serves as a basis for planning to intervene in the family.

An Intervention Methodology

Let us now look at the second or "doing" dimension of an approach to pastoral family therapy, an intervention methodology. I like to think of the family therapist as performing five types of activity: (1) joining the family as a temporary though effective member, (2) assessing the family's problem, (3) planning and contracting with the family for change, (4) implementing the plan for change, and (5) leaving the family while helping them integrate the changes made. Each of these activities merits separate consideration.

Therapeutic Activities

These five activities can be thought of as clusters of therapist skills. They can also be thought of as stages of any particular therapy session or of the overall therapy process, though they should not be viewed as always following each other in unvariable sequence. As we look at each of the five activities, we will be applying to them the principles and techniques of this book.

Joining the Family

In order to be able to facilitate change in a family, clergy or lay therapists must first be accepted into the family. I use the plural *therapists* because it is often an advantage to have cotherapists facing the powerfully organized system of the family in order to impact it without being so absorbed into it as to lose therapist influence.*

The therapists open the family meeting by making a warm, human contact with each family member, greeting them by name and individualized comment, much as one welcomes guests into the home. The pastor may have the advantage of being able to build upon social relationships established with the family in previous visits to their home. However, whether the therapists already have a relationship with the family or not, it is important for them to begin the meeting with a period of relaxed social conversation that allows the helpers to become involved with each family member.

The most crucial dimension of joining the family is learning the family's language and beginning to use it in talking to the family. Therapists listen for how family members define themselves and their beliefs about reality, their metaphors and myths. Family therapists are like anthropologists in that they seek to learn and join into the culture they have come to study.

Observation skills are thus essential to this joining skill-cluster area. Therapists discover family metaphors through observing key words repeated by family members, especially picture words. For instance, in the illustration in chapter 3 Pastor Evans heard Mary frequently talking about "burden." Therapists also discover family metaphors by paying attention to the way family members act with each other in the room. Family members literally perform a living metaphoric portrait of their family life by the ways they choose to sit in the room, talk with each other, and act toward each other. For example, in the Baker family at the beginning of this chapter, when the parents began to argue with each other the boys jabbed each other and Teresa knocked over the stand, drawing everyone's attention onto herself. This may have been a metaphor expressing how the Baker family avoids conflict by deflecting the tension onto Teresa or the other children. This series of acts performed before Pastor Taylor may be a recurring pattern or a significant family metaphor. The pastor would need to watch to see if it continues to be repeated.

As the therapists learn the family's language and world-view beliefs, they begin to use them in talking to the family members. The more this occurs, the more the family feels understood and attended to by the therapists and the more willing the family becomes to attend to and be open to the therapists' suggestions to them.*

While therapists join the family by being friendly and attentive, they need also to join in a manner that makes them clearly the leaders of the session. Carl Whitaker believes that family therapy begins with a "battle for structure" in which members vie with therapists to see who will determine such structural matters as the time of the meeting, who will be present at it, and how the meeting will proceed.† If therapists win this battle by demonstrating they are clearly in charge the family members will trust their strength and subsequently give them authority to influence the family's metaphoric structure through therapeutic interventions. If the therapists don't take charge the family is likely to remain unchanged. In the illustration with the Baker family Pastor Taylor yielded his leadership by allowing (*a*) the family to determine when the meeting began, (*b*) Mrs. Baker to determine who would do the talking, and (*c*) the children to act as they chose.

Assessing the Problem

After making all the family members feel welcomed and at ease the therapists exercise leadership by asking each member in turn to describe what they believe to be the problems that have brought them to the meeting. When the therapists have heard from each member, they encourage all the members to begin talking with each other about the problems. This frees the helpers to step back and clearly observe the ways family members interact with each other. At this time the therapists may see the family's problems displayed in behavioral metaphors. Some of the behavioral interaction will be analogous to the verbal descriptions the family members have given of their problems. Difficulties occurring between children may be metaphors for difficulties that exist between their parents.

On the basis of their observations the therapists now begin to form in their own minds a tentative assessment of the family's problem. An assessment is made by applying the therapists' conceptual framework to the information gathered from the family. The therapists particularly focus upon where the family may be blocked developmentally in the life cycle and how they may be blocked by their repeating patterns of behavior.

For example, a tentative assessment of the Baker family might include that the family is blocked at the "letting people grow" stage of the family life cycle by patterns of avoiding conflict which are not allowing adult and child family members to develop a secure sense of identity. The core problem needing attention may be the behavioral metaphor that when the parents begin to argue the children act in distracting ways until they get the parents' attention.

This beginning assessment is usually not shared with the

family. The therapists will need to test such initial hypotheses as they continue to interact with and observe the family.

Planning and Contracting for Change

All the family members having discussed the problems, the therapists now ask them to pull together what problem or problems the family members want to resolve through therapy. The therapists assist the members to define problems in a form that is operational, that is, describing behavior that can be observed, counted, or measured so that the family will be able to know when a problem is resolved. For example, if the Bakers defined as problems "childhood antagonism" or "family disharmony" these problem definitions would be too vague to be useful. A better formulation would be "the children fighting with each other daily," because everyone would be able to observe a change in the occurrence of this behavior.*

When the problems to be focused upon have been defined the therapists contract with the family members to work together toward the goal of the problems' resolution. The statement of the contract needs to be in the language of the family and to be clear and specific enough so the family will know when the goal has been reached. Understanding also needs to be reached with the family as to what part will be played by the therapists and by the family members. For instance, therapists will agree to lead the sessions and offer family members feedback and suggestions, while family members will agree to try out new actions during the session and as homework assignments between meetings. Family members thus agree to become participants in their own healing. Ongoing planning for the sessions is done by the therapists toward achieving the contracted goals. Therapists plan interventions that are aimed at influencing both the problem details specified by the family and the family metaphors that appear to be blocking the family's development.

Implementing the Plan for Change

In planning and carrying out interventions, clergy or lay family therapists may make use of any of the techniques of metaphoric communication I have defined. Examples using each of

the techniques in therapy are given in the description of Pastor
Evans's work described in chapter 3. I want here to elaborate on
only two of the techniques that are of particular importance for
family therapy: action imperative and story.

Action imperatives are particularly useful in family therapy
for impacting the behavioral metaphors that a family is enacting.
When the therapists have identified repetitious sequences of actions the family is performing they may interrupt these actions
and ask the family members to change their behavior at that
moment in the session. The therapists may also give the members homework assignments to further carry out the changed
behavior. Such interventions themselves are metaphors through
which the therapists are communicating to the family how to
behave in order to experience a different outcome.*

For example, therapists might identify the Baker family's sequence of Mr. and Mrs. Baker interrupting each other, arguing,
and then being distracted by the children. The therapists would
then interrupt the family and institute a rule for the remainder
of the session: only one person can talk at a time and that person may not be interrupted unless he or she chooses to give
someone else the floor.

Another action imperative would be to have one therapist
take the children to another room while the remaining therapist
instructs the parents to discuss the issue of how to respond to
the children's fighting. With the children unavailable to distract
them the parents would be encouraged to keep working at the
issue until they reach an agreement.

Both of these interventions could be tried. Both could also be
assigned to the Bakers to continue doing at home between
sessions.

Another very useful family therapy technique is telling stories.
Therapists can relate to a family how other families struggled
with similar problems and resolved them. Such stories stimulate
hope in the family that they too can change, while also suggesting new directions that the family can explore.

A further therapeutic skill is constructing new stories that fit
unique needs and goals of particular families who come for therapy. In his book *Therapeutic Metaphors* David Gordon has de-

scribed in detail how to construct such stories.* Briefly summarized, Gordon lists the following steps for developing a story: (1) Select an imaginary setting for the story. (2) Choose story characters that represent each person significantly involved in the problem, with the relationships between characters parallel to the relationships between the family members (such as father and son being represented by a ship's captain and cabin boy). (3) Invent a sequence of events for the story that parallels the actions that occur sequentially in the family's problem. (4) Plan an event in the story that shows a way to break up the old repetitive pattern involved in the family's problem. (5) Phrase for one or more of the characters a response that suggests both an understanding of the old pattern and an intuition of a way of undoing the old pattern. (6) Invent a climactic action for the story that metaphorically serves as a bridge between current problems of the family and their desired outcome goal in therapy. Gordon believes that family members themselves may give the therapists suggestions for the content of this bridging action by describing how they are currently blocking themselves from getting to the goal. Either what they are avoiding doing or what they are trying too hard to do may be blocking them. (7) Tell the story to the family, making use of reframing and special language patterns such as nonreferring phrases. Leaving the solution phrased in such nonspecific language places upon the metaphoric minds of the family members the responsibility to translate the story's messages into meanings that fit for their lives.

To illustrate this story-building process, I will outline a story that could be prepared for the Baker family, indicating by number the stages of the construction process being illustrated.

(1) Deep in the forest lived a family of deer, including (2) a fine stag, a lovely doe, two strong young bucks, and a tiny, mischievous fawn. (3) One morning the stag and doe stood in the middle of a clearing planning what route to take for their journey that day. They fell into bickering with each other so that the day began to pass without their being aware of it. The two bucks, in order to pass the time, began testing out their newly forming horns by butting each other. While everyone was thus occupied the fawn slipped away into the forest and became

lost. (4) When the stag and the doe discovered she was missing they abruptly stopped their bickering. (5) The doe said, "While we have stood here arguing the children have had no leadership and one of them has gotten lost." The stag replied, "You are right. We must now act quickly and together." (6) Swiftly the stag and the doe devised with the two bucks a search plan that used all their individual resources: the stag's experienced knowledge of the terrain, the doe's intuition of where a young fawn might wander, and the bucks' sharp eyes and speed afoot. They enacted their plan, and within an hour they discovered the fawn splashing in a small pond. (7) Sighing with relief, the stag said wisely, "In finding someone precious who was lost I believe we may have found something else that we had lost." "Yes," added the doe, "I think today we have all learned something of importance."

Leaving the Family and Integrating Changes

At the beginning of this discussion of the process of "doing" family therapy, I emphasized the importance of therapists effectively joining families. At the end of the therapy process it is equally important that therapists effectively *leave* the families so that family members can continue to take responsibility for their own lives.

As an analogy for family therapy, Andrew Ferber suggests viewing the family as a ship on a long voyage and the therapists as consultants who fly in by helicopter. After inspecting the ship and crew these consultants suggest some changes for the voyage, ship, and relationships among crew members and then fly away in their helicopter while the ship continues its voyage.*

I believe this analogy underscores the temporary quality of therapists' membership in a family they seek to help. Therapists can foster this temporary quality all the way through the therapy process by continually asking family members to participate in their own healing through carrying out activities. This encourages families to feel that they, not the therapists, have been responsible for the changes they experience. Therapists can also stimulate family members' sense of responsibility by the use of metaphoric communication techniques that place the responsibility for change clearly upon the metaphoric minds of the family members.

In the closing session of a family therapy process, therapists may help the members to integrate changes through rational-mind reflection and commitment to ongoing growth activity. A family can be asked to discuss together three questions: (1) What problems did we first come here to resolve? (2) What changes have we made toward resolving those problems? (3) What activities do we still need to continue in order to further resolve the problems? It is often helpful to have the family members commit themselves to specific plans of action for furthering their growth process.

Finally, therapists can facilitate family members integrating any transformation of family metaphors with their spiritual interpretation of the meaning of their lives. A good focusing question for this purpose is, How are our belief systems changed by these changes in our family? The therapists and family may join in a closing prayer of thanksgiving to the Holy Spirit for his transforming activity in their midst.

Counseling a family is a complex activity. A pastor or lay leader who wishes to counsel a family in the way I have described in this chapter is well advised to undertake specialized training in family therapy. Pastors and laypersons may obtain valuable supervision and training by contacting members of national accrediting bodies in the fields of pastoral counseling and family therapy.* Another potentially useful avenue for the pastor is to do cotherapy with trained family therapists who are members of the church or colleagues in the ministry. A pastor-lay cotherapy team can offer families a particularly valuable opportunity for transforming old metaphors into metaphors rich in meaning and possibility for their lives.

Epilogue: The Three Little Pigs Revisited

Years had passed since the crisis with the wolf. The family of three little pigs had settled down comfortably in their brick house in the suburbs. Gradually boredom had set in. Each of the little pigs felt empty. One day they decided that what they were missing had to do with love, and they determined to go and seek love's meaning.

The first little pig went to the library and read all he could on the subject of love. When he finished he had learned a great deal but still felt empty.

The second little pig read in the newspaper that a famous pig was coming to town to deliver a series of lectures on the topic of love. This second little pig attended all the lectures and was filled with enthusiasm. His emotional high lasted four days. After that his life was pretty much what it was before.

The third little pig invited two other pig families over to their house one evening. All three families began sharing their life stories and continued late into the night. They found this so interesting that they decided to meet like this regularly. After several months they discovered that they knew and cared about each other deeply.

One evening after the other families had left, the third little pig spoke to the others. "Now I know what love is," he said, "for I have experienced it."

In this book I have attempted to show how family change occurs through Spirit-empowered communication directed to the metaphoric minds of family members. This communication results in family members having new experiences of each other, experiences that lead to the creation of new family metaphors.

The Holy Spirit effects this transformation of metaphors within the context of a caring community of families. Many families today are searching for such experiences of community. Our society's families tend to be isolated from each other. They exist in a variety of forms. These families hunger for intimate connection with other families. Additionally, men and women within families are struggling to discover their identities as sexual beings within a societal context characterized by rapidly changing metaphors defining masculinity and femininity. In such a society the church has unprecedented opportunity to be a community of caring support and honest dialogue within which family members can sort out the meaning of their life stories.

A former seminary professor of mine, Dr. Gerhard Frost, told me recently of a colleague's experience when visiting Africa. He drove over a hill at dusk and saw ahead a series of fires stretching across the plain. As he drove near he discovered that each fire was a campfire in the center of a village. Around the fire gathered all the tribe's families, telling and retelling the stories of the tribe. Dr. Frost concluded, "This is a good model for the church—the community of the story."

I want to encourage churches to gather their families around campfires and fireplaces to share their stories. In such rich, late-night sharings families can learn from others how they have gotten through a life cycle passage, and families can nourish and strengthen each other for the journey.

While I have limited my discussion of churches' ministry to families to family enrichment, education, and therapy, the principles and techniques I have described can be applied much more widely in congregational life. The sermon, corporate worship, and pastoral home visitation are some of the areas in which metaphoric-mind communication is particularly relevant.* Through these and other means all of us can assist the church in becoming "the community of the story."

Notes

Page

2. *Idries Shah, "The Tale of the Sands," in *Tales of the Dervishes* (New York: E. P. Dutton and Co., 1970), pp. 23–24.

3. *Donald Meichenbaum, "Self-instructional Methods," in *Helping People Change*, ed. Frederick H. Kanfer and Arnold P. Goldstein (New York: Pergamon Press, 1975), p. 388.

3. †Paul Watzlawick, *The Language of Change* (New York: Basic Books, 1978).

5. *Bob Samples, *The Metaphoric Mind: A Celebration of Creative Consciousness* (Reading, Mass.: Addison-Wesley Publishing Co., 1976), p. 19.

5. †Ibid., pp. 143–44, 189–90.

7. *John B. Cobb, Jr., *Theology and Pastoral Care* (Philadelphia: Fortress Press, 1977), pp. 25–32.

12. *John Ernest and Allen Saunders, "Mary Worth," *Seattle Times*, 5 February 1977.

12. †Evelyn Millis Duvall, *Marriage and Family Development*, 5th ed. (Philadelphia: J. B. Lippincott Co., 1977); Jay Haley, *Uncommon Therapy: The Psychiatric Techniques of Milton H. Erickson, M.D.* (New York: W. W. Norton and Co., 1973), pp. 41–64; Michael A. Solomon, "A Developmental, Conceptual Premise for Family Therapy," *Family Process* 12, 2 (June 1973): 179–88.

19. *Duvall, *Family Development*, p. 347.

27. *Methods of teaching relaxation are described in Robert A. Anderson, *Stress Power!* (New York: Human Sciences Press, 1978), pp. 155–68; Herbert Benson, *The Relaxation Response* (New York: William Morrow and Co., 1976), esp. pp. 114–15; and Kanfer and Goldstein, eds., *Helping People Change*, pp. 415–18. See also in this series the volume by Howard W. Stone, *Using Behavioral Methods in Pastoral Counseling* (Philadelphia: Fortress Press, 1980), pp. 17–20.

28. *John A. Sanford, *Healing and Wholeness* (New York: Paulist Press, 1977), pp. 140–48.

28. †Richard Bandler and John Grinder, *Patterns of the Hypnotic Techniques of Milton H. Erickson, M.D.* (Cupertino, Calif.: META Publications, 1975), 1: 185–89.

29. *Watzlawick, *Language of Change,* pp. 61–63.
29. †Richard Bandler and John Grinder, *The Structure of Magic* (Palo Alto, Calif.: Science and Behavior Books, 1975), 1: 169.
29. ‡Carl Fellner, "The Use of Teaching Stories in Conjoint Family Therapy," *Family Process* 15, 4 (December 1976): 427–31. I recommend reading his entire article.
30. *John Grinder, Judith DeLozier, and Richard Bandler, *Patterns of the Hypnotic Techniques of Milton H. Erickson, M.D.* (Cupertino, Calif.: META Publications, 1977), 2: 59–62.
31. *Sanford, *Healing and Wholeness,* p. 153.
31. †Ibid., p. 156.
31. ‡Bandler and Grinder, *Structure of Magic,* 1: 164–66; 2: 13.
32. *Watzlawick, *Language of Change,* pp. 118–26. See also Paul Watzlawick, John Weakland, and Richard Fisch, *Change* (New York: W. W. Norton and Co., 1974), pp. 92–109.
33. *William A. Miller, *When Going to Pieces Holds You Together* (Minneapolis: Augsburg Publishing House, 1976).
33. †Watzlawick, *Language of Change,* p. 74.
34. *Bandler and Grinder, *Patterns,* 1: 24–25, 239–40.
35. *Grinder, DeLozier, and Bandler, *Patterns,* 2: 53–55, 69, 110.
36. *Watzlawick, *Language of Change,* pp. 128–32.
36. †Ibid., pp. 69–73.
39. *For a description of this movement see Herbert A. Otto, ed., *Marriage and Family Enrichment: New Perspectives and Programs* (Nashville: Abingdon Press, 1976).
40. *Reuben Hill, *Family Development in Three Generations: A Longitudinal Study of Changing Family Patterns of Planning and Achievement* (Cambridge, Mass.: Schenkman Publishing Co., 1970), p. 334.
41. *David Mace and Vera Mace, "Marriage Enrichment through Group Interaction," mimeographed (Winston-Salem, N.C., April 1972), p. 5.
41. †See Margaret Sawin, *Family Enrichment through Family Clusters* (Valley Forge: Judson Press, 1979).
44. *O. Carl Simonton, Stephanie Matthews-Simonton, and James Creighton, *Getting Well Again* (Los Angeles: J. P. Tarcher, 1978), pp. 164–72.
45. *This tale is told by Fellner in "Teaching Stories," pp. 430–31.
47. *David Ireland, *Letters to an Unborn Child* (New York: Harper and Row, 1974), p. 68.
50. *See especially Sherod Miller, Elam W. Nunnally, and Daniel B. Wackman, *Alive and Aware* (Minneapolis: Interpersonal Communication Programs, 1975); and John Powell, *The Secret of Staying in Love* (Niles, Ill.: Argus Communications, 1974).
55. *For marriage enrichment training write: Association of Couples for Marriage Enrichment, 459 South Church Street, P. O. Box 10596, Winston-Salem, North Carolina 27108. For family enrichment training write: Family Clustering, Inc., P. O. Box 8452, Twelve Corners Branch, Rochester, New York 14618.

59. *For much of the format of this program I am indebted to the work of Philip Abrego and Lawrence Brammer at the University of Washington, Seattle. See their publication "Developing Coping Skills for Career-Related Change" (Palo Alto, Calif.: American Institute for Research, 1979).

60. *Marjorie F. Lowenthal et al., *Four Stages of Life: A Comparative Study of Women and Men Facing Transitions* (San Francisco: Jossey-Bass Publishers, 1975).

61. *John Adams, John Hayes, and Barrie Hopson, *Transitions: Understanding and Managing Personal Change* (Montclair, N.J.: Allanheld, Osmun, and Co., 1977), esp. pp. 8–13.

63. *Watzlawick, *Language of Change*, p. 61. See also Simonton, *Getting Well Again*, pp. 129–37.

63. †Anderson, *Stress Power!* pp. 214–15.

65. *Nikolai Gogol, *The Collected Tales and Plays of Nikolai Gogol*, ed. Leonard J. Kent, trans. Constance Garnett (New York: Pantheon Books, 1964).

65. *For descriptions of these processes see Abrego and Brammer, "Developing Coping Skills"; also Irving L. Janis and Leonard Mann, *Decision Making* (New York: The Free Press, 1977), esp. pp. 405–14.

67. *See above, pp. 54–56.

70. *Augustus Napier and Carl Whitaker, "Problems of the Beginning Family Therapist," in *Techniques of Family Psychotherapy: A Primer*, ed. Donald A. Bloch (New York: Grune and Stratton, 1973), p. 120.

72. *See Augustus Napier and Carl Whitaker, "A Conversation about Co-Therapy," in *The Book of Family Therapy*, ed. Andrew Ferber, Marilyn Mendelsohn, and Augustus Napier (Boston: Houghton Mifflin Co., 1973), pp. 480–504.

73. *Milton H. Erickson, Ernest L. Rossi, and Sheila I. Rossi, *Hypnotic Realities* (New York: Irvington Publishers, 1976), pp. 15–17.

73. †Napier and Whitaker, "Beginning Family Therapist," p. 110.

75. *See Jay Haley, *Problem-Solving Therapy* (San Francisco: Jossey-Bass Publishers, 1976), pp. 40–43.

76. *Ibid., pp. 65–66, 88–90.

77. *David Gordon, *Therapeutic Metaphors* (Cupertino, Calif.: META Publications, 1978), pp. 40–50.

78. *Ferber, *Family Therapy*, p. 562.

79. *For information regarding supervision and training available in your area write: American Association of Pastoral Counselors, 3 West Twenty-ninth Street, New York, New York 10001; and American Association for Marriage and Family Therapy, 924 West Ninth Street, Upland, California 91786.

81. *A fascinating application of the sermon is made by John L. Topolewski, "The Rabbi's Elixir: Epistemology and Story Telling," *Nexus 56* 22, 1 (Fall 1978): 8–16. See also Edmund A. Steimle, Morris J. Niedenthal, and Charles L. Rice, *Preaching the Story* (Philadelphia: Fortress Press, 1980).

Annotated Bibliography

Beavers, W. Robert. *Psychotherapy and Growth: A Family Systems Perspective.* New York: Brunner/Mazel, 1977. This excellent description of systems theory and the nature of psychotherapy includes a lucid presentation of research results identifying characteristics of the *healthy* family, which renders it invaluable for goal setting in educational as well as therapeutic settings.

Cooper, John Charles. *Fantasy and the Human Spirit.* New York: Seabury Press, 1975. A theologian's imaginative development of the thesis that our personal religion is shaped by the particular life story we are telling ourselves.

Duvall, Evelyn Millis. *Marriage and Family Development.* 5th ed. Philadelphia: J. B. Lippincott Co., 1977. An introduction to family development theory and a detailed description of the stages of the family life cycle.

Gordon, David. *Therapeutic Metaphors.* Cupertino, Calif.: META Publications, 1978. A very readable yet carefully detailed and illustrated explanation of techniques of metaphoric communication.

Haley, Jay. *Problem-Solving Therapy.* San Francisco: Jossey-Bass Publishers, 1976. Gives a clear, organized approach to how to do family therapy, with special attention to the use of action imperatives.

—————. *Uncommon Therapy: The Psychiatric Techniques of Milton H. Erickson, M.D.* New York: W. W. Norton and Co., 1973. The first two chapters are a concise, fascinating introduction to Erickson's approach to therapy and the family life cycle.

Levinson, Daniel J. *The Seasons of a Man's Life*. New York: Alfred A. Knopf, 1978. A substantive rendering of the sequential tasks of the adult life cycle.

Otto, Herbert A., ed. *Marriage and Family Enrichment: New Perspectives and Programs*. Nashville: Abingdon Press, 1976. A practical volume with numerous descriptions of actual enrichment programs.

Samuels, Mike, and Samuels, Nancy. *Seeing with the Mind's Eye: The History, Techniques, and Uses of Visualization*. New York: Random House, 1975. An exceptionally thorough guide to metaphoric-mind practices of imagination and visualization.

Sanford, John A. *Healing and Wholeness*. New York: Paulist Press, 1977. Metaphoric-mind communication approaches from Jungian and pastoral perspectives.

Sawin, Margaret. *Family Enrichment through Family Clusters*. Valley Forge: Judson Press, 1979. Packed with practical descriptions of how to do family enrichment and resource references for leaders, by the pioneer of the family clustering movement in the church.

Watzlawick, Paul. *The Language of Change*. New York: Basic Books, 1978. Valuable introduction to metaphoric-mind communication theory and application to psychotherapy.